The Essence of
BHAGWAD GITA

Atul Sehgal is a New Delhi based author of *Happiness All the Way*. He has a long association with the Arya Samaj, and is a keen proponent of Vedic ideology. Articles on motivation and spirituality, written by Mr Sehgal, have been published by *Hindustan Times* and *The New Indian Express*.

He can be contacted at: atul4956@gmail.com

The Essence of
BHAGWAD GITA
70 Verses at Its Core

ATUL SEHGAL

Published by
Rupa Publications India Pvt. Ltd 2018
7/16, Ansari Road, Daryaganj
New Delhi 110002

Sales centres:
Prayagraj Bengaluru Chennai
Hyderabad Jaipur Kathmandu
Kolkata Mumbai

Copyright © Atul Sehgal, 2018

The views and opinions expressed in this book are the author's own and the facts are as reported by him which have been verified to the extent possible, and the publishers are not in any way liable for the same.

All rights reserved.
No part of this publication may be reproduced, transmitted, or stored in a retrieval system, in any form or by any means, electronic, mechanical, photocopying, recording or otherwise, without the prior permission of the publisher.

P-ISBN: 978-81-291-5104-9
E-ISBN: 978-81-291-5105-6

Second impression 2023

10 9 8 7 6 5 4 3 2

The moral right of the author has been asserted.

Printed in India

This book is sold subject to the condition that it shall not, by way of trade or otherwise, be lent, resold, hired out, or otherwise circulated, without the publisher's prior consent, in any form of binding or cover other than that in which it is published.

*To my mother, late Pushpa Sehgal,
for sowing in me the seeds of spirituality*

Contents

Foreword — xi
Preface — xiii

Chapter 1	Attachment	1
Chapter 2	Mental Perversion	5
Chapter 3	Self-control	8
Chapter 4	True Knowledge	11
Chapter 5	The Mortal Body	15
Chapter 6	Dispel the Doubt	19
Chapter 7	Soul is the Master of the Body	22
Chapter 8	The Immortality of the Soul	25
Chapter 9	Duty is Religion	28
Chapter 10	The Twin Benefits of Duty	32
Chapter 11	The Eternal Law of Karma	36
Chapter 12	Mental Fortitude, Intellectual Clarity	39
Chapter 13	Composed Intellect	42
Chapter 14	Stability of the Intellect	46
Chapter 15	The Demise of Desire	49
Chapter 16	Perspective of a Yogi	53
Chapter 17	The Virtues of Yagya	56
Chapter 18	The Fruits of Yagya	59
Chapter 19	The Importance of Varnadharma	63

Chapter 20	The Past Connection	67
Chapter 21	Reincarnation for Divine Purpose	70
Chapter 22	Birth and Life of a Yogi	74
Chapter 23	Right Knowledge, Right Action	77
Chapter 24	Mental Equanimity: The Key to Liberation	81
Chapter 25	The Yagya Performer	84
Chapter 26	Knowledge and Evolution	87
Chapter 27	Renunciation and Righteous Action	90
Chapter 28	The Yoga of Knowledge	94
Chapter 29	Self-help	98
Chapter 30	Elevating the Self	101
Chapter 31	The Yogic Pose	104
Chapter 32	We are All Alike	107
Chapter 33	The Power of Divine Connection	110
Chapter 34	The Primordial Elements of the Almighty	113
Chapter 35	The Primary Cause and Basis of All	116
Chapter 36	Core and Crux	119
Chapter 37	Modes of Manifestation	122
Chapter 38	The Essence of Everything	125
Chapter 39	Who Worships Him?	128
Chapter 40	The Support of the Almighty	132
Chapter 41	The Last Moments	136
Chapter 42	The Aphorism of Salvation	139
Chapter 43	The Technique of Meditation	143
Chapter 44	The Knowledge of Deliverance	147
Chapter 45	Seeing God in Everything	151
Chapter 46	Offer Everything to Him	154
Chapter 47	Understanding Him Further	158
Chapter 48	His Greatness	161
Chapter 49	Comprehending His Attributes	165
Chapter 50	The Best Among All	169
Chapter 51	More Allegories	172

Chapter 52	Identity Patterns	176
Chapter 53	Know Him Further	179
Chapter 54	His Opulence	182
Chapter 55	The Divine Revelation	185
Chapter 56	Seeing the Invisible	188
Chapter 57	Description of the Divine	191
Chapter 58	The Tide of Destiny	194
Chapter 59	The Divine Writ	197
Chapter 60	The Lord's Cosmic Form	200
Chapter 61	Exposition of His Greatness	203
Chapter 62	Unattached Karma for Salvation	206
Chapter 63	Scientific Explanation of God	209
Chapter 64	Illuminator of its Zone	212
Chapter 65	The Scientific Basis of Human Karma	216
Chapter 66	The Effects of the Three Attributes	219
Chapter 67	Transcending the Range of Gunas	222
Chapter 68	Definition of the Saint	225
Chapter 69	Pathway to the Ultimate Abode	228
Chapter 70	The Final Sermon	232
Epilogue		235
Acknowledgements		237

Foreword

Shri Atul Sehgal has been writing extensively on the subjects of motivation and spirituality for quite some time. Being intimately affiliated with the Arya Samaj, Shri Sehgal has been an active exponent of the pristine Vedic ideology, and this fact is clearly visible in his writings.

The Hindu scripture Bhagwadgita (or the Gita) is widely read, interpreted and followed as a guide to happy living, as a textual key to spiritual transcendence of man. Its followers have claimed it to be a beacon of light to help man trudge safely through the jungle of life, which is marked by uncertainties, miseries and difficulties of all kinds.

The Essence of Bhagwadgita is a unique effort to bring out the divine message of the scripture through Vedic interpretation and explanation. The author has explained the meaning and import of the core seventy verses of the scripture in a most lucid manner and described how the message of each verse can be applied to contemporary life situations for the betterment of human life. Drawing upon practical situations of modern living, the author has demonstrated very well the perfect applicability of the verses of the Bhagwadgita to today's world.

This work will do a lot to reinforce human faith in the divine Creator and enable today's global citizens to acquire a clearer understanding of the purpose of life and the application of eternal tools of spirituality to enhance human happiness and fulfilment. This will also go a long way in stemming ideological confusion prevalent today. I compliment the author for his efforts and am sure that the book will prove to be a valuable guide for contemporary humans for greater fulfilment in the eternal journey called life.

I extend my best wishes to him.

Dr Punam Suri
Recipient of the Padma Shri
President, Arya Pradeshik Pratinidhi Sabha
Managing Editor, *The Daily Milap*

Preface

The famed scripture of the yore, Bhagwadgita, is widely read and followed by a large section of human community, not only in India, the land of its origin, but across the world. This ancient text serves as a beacon of light to the ordinary human beings struggling through the course of their mundane existence and to the more distinctive persons seeking the answers to the riddles of life and in quest of the higher truths of existence.

The Bhagwadgita, as a scriptural text, is generally available as a compendium of seven hundred verses which are believed to be delivered by Shri Krishna to Arjun at Kurukshetra, the battlefield of the great war between the armies of Kauravs and Pandavs, more than 5,000 years ago. The entire text is in the form of these verses in which Shri Krishna, the legendary figure of the epic Mahabharat, exhorts Arjun, the key warrior of the Pandavs, to discharge his duty and fight his enemy pitched against him, even if some of the warriors in his enemy camp include his dear cousins, friends or revered preceptor. The Bhagwadgita (the song divine) is a discourse from the enlightened, erudite master of Yoga, Shri Krishna, who is believed to be God incarnate. Hence, the version of Bhagwadgita that we have today is believed to be a collection of verses uttered by the Lord of the universe, and its correctness and completeness is ensured by the Lord for human posterity.

The above statements have to be seen in the light of true knowledge of physical and spiritual entities inhabiting the universe. They need to be checked against the metaphysical realities expounded in the Vedas—the eternal scriptures of humankind—referred to in the Bhagwadgita itself. The four Vedas, viz. Rigveda, Yajurveda, Samveda and Atharvaveda, are widely acknowledged as primeval scriptures of mankind and talk of three primordial entities existing in the universe. These are—the inert matter, the countless living souls and one animate infinite spiritual entity called God who creates the material universe from inert matter, controls it and dissolves it, and this sequential process of creation, regulation and dissolution goes on eternally.

God is formless, infinite, omniscient and omnipotent. Hence, as per the Vedas, he cannot, need not and does not incarnate as a human for any purpose whatsoever. Therefore, to regard Shri Krishna as God incarnate is fundamentally incorrect, as it goes against the tenets of the Vedas which even the Bhagwadgita regards as the words of God and eternal, inviolable truths. In the opinion of many proponents of the original Vedic religion, the Bhagwadgita of seven hundred verses that we see today is actually not the original Bhagwadgita but a grossly enlarged version of the original, which contained only seventy verses. They believe that sometime after the battle of Mahabharat, scholars of Sanskrit inserted additional verses into the original Bhagwadgita. If that be true, there could have been many reasons for this. But whatever were the reasons, the originality of the sacred text was surely vitiated.

Some of the Vedic scholars believe that some 2,500 years ago in history, the priestly class wanted to deify Shri Krishna and install his idols in temples. Idol worship had already taken roots and this superstitious practice was attended by the offerings of money and food by human devotees to the idols of their deity installed at the temples. The food and money enriched the temple caretakers and priests. Our scriptures were also in the custody of these priests and scholars who were free to carry out changes in the scriptural texts. The priestly class to which the above scholars belonged had probably grown overly materialistic and this led to the interpolations to our great scriptural book.

Religion is meant for bringing peace, progress and bliss to the human society. And religion is rooted in the scriptures. All scriptures are sourced to the omniscient Creator. The medium of transmission of divine life-elevating knowledge are scholarly sages and enlightened seers. Ordinary humans, being inherently imperfect of knowledge and understanding, are liable to misinterpret or misrepresent the strands of original divine knowledge. Shri Krishna was an enlightened human who had a complete understanding of the Vedas, and anything that he uttered could not be contradictory to the Vedas. The Vedas clearly describe God as a formless, infinite and spiritual entity who is never born and never incarnates as a human. The Vedas also denounce idol worship as a regressive practice. They categorically pronounce that idol worship never elevates a man spiritually but brings his downfall.

That the Bhagwadgita of seventy verses could actually be the original text is corroborated by the fact that it is the collection of sermons delivered by Shri Krishna to Arjun pitched in the war against the army of Kauravs at Kurukshetra, almost 5,100 years ago in history. Shri Krishna exhorts Arjun not to get overwhelmed by the sight of his kith and kin in the enemy camp and perform his solemn duty to fight against the enemy as a Kshatriya. It seems absolutely improbable and unrealistic that Shri Krishna had delivered sermons to Arjun in the form of as many as seven hundred verses. Warriors in those days assembled at the battleground fifteen minutes before sunrise, the ruled time of commencement of battle. Uttering so many verses would have taken three hours. Where was the time for the huge armies to wait for so long before commencing the battle?

It is with the above logical understanding that this book has been written against the backdrop of the supposedly original Bhagwadgita of seventy verses. This original scriptural text is understood to have been transported by Hindu immigrants to the islands of Java and Bali nearly 2,000 years ago. Historical transcripts, which were found, indicated that this text was available in those islands in AD 535. In AD 1438, the original texts available in Java were transported to Bali. The text was retrieved by a subsequent Hindu visitor to Bali in AD 1912.

It is considered necessary to reiterate that true knowledge is the prime vehicle for human progress, since this knowledge is sourced originally to the creator of man and the preserver of the material universe. This underlines the great importance of sorting out grain from the chaff. Scriptures are the guiding light for humanity, and since human beings are innately of limited knowledge, they need to have original scriptures based on true knowledge by their side to advance further in the tumultuous journey called life. Writing this book is a humble step towards that end purpose.

The seventy verses on which this work is based are a part of the existing Bhagwadgita of seven hundred verses, and these seventy verses cover the entire philosophy of the existing Bhagwadgita. Hence, this book could be considered as the essence of the Bhagwadgita without loss of the above purpose.

In this book, an attempt has been made to explain the import of each important verse of the Bhagwadgita in the context of contemporary human civilization. Examples from modern-life situations, relevant to each verse, have been liberally provided to bring out the application of the verse to human life—to enrich life and make it more worthwhile. It is hoped that the book will provide the much needed direction towards multifaceted progress to modern-day human beings who are grappling with multiple problems, and will enable them to derive far greater fulfilment in their precious lives.

Chapter 1

Attachment

Drishtavemam swajanam Krishna yuyutsum samupasthitam,
Na cha shrayo-anupashyami hatwa swajan mahavey,
Na kankshe vijayam Krishna na cha rajyam sukhani cha.

Arjun: O Krishna! I am greatly pained to see my kith and kin assembled here. I wonder what I am going to gain by slaying them in this battle. I am going to do no good to myself by killing my kinsmen. Dear Krishna! I hardly cherish victory and the spoils of victory in such a battle.

Attachment is a sense of passionate belongingness. This belongingness is false, as it is based on wrong understanding. The truth is that nothing in this world belongs to us. We are all temporary travellers here, having brought nothing with us at birth and will take nothing with us when we depart. Our relationships will cease to be immediately at death. Our duties must consider the tenets of dharma or righteousness. We have an obligation to maintain peace and harmony in the world. Our every action should be conducive to maintenance of this peace and harmony and preservation of the purity of our physical environment. At the same time, we should do everything in consistency with our true purpose of living.

Arjun tells Shri Krishna that he, as a warrior, is overawed by the prospect of slaying his kinsmen with his own hands. The Kaurav cousins, with whom he had grown up, playing and studying together; the revered teacher Dronacharya; and the respected grandfather Bhishma were all in his enemy camp. The prospect of fighting them and killing them started weighing heavily on him. His attachment with his kinsmen came in the way of the performance of his duty as a Kshatriya warrior.

Attachment blinds us to the core realities of life. Attachment to wealth creates an obsession for it which generates monetary greed which, in turn, perverts a person's moral conduct. Attachment to other physical assets, like property, vehicles, bullion or other valuables, creates a constant concern for their preservation, besides a nagging urge to acquire more. This makes us restless and ill at ease. We do not understand the hard reality that none of these assets are our own. We are mere custodians of them as long as we live. These physical entities are owned by the Master of the universe who created it. Once we depart, we are going to take nothing with us, not even their memories. Why? Because we are not physical bodies, but souls. Our real need is not food or money or houses but emancipation and bliss. We must look at our material passions from this very realistic angle. Being temporary custodians of our physical possessions, our duty is to preserve and use them in the best possible manner for the good of the family, community and nation. How we handle our assets, how much benefit will accrue to others through our actions involving our assets and the qualitative aspects of those actions are more important. These actions are our true wealth which will accompany us in the life hereafter.

In this world, we humans are continuously living in connections and affiliations. We have filial, professional or friendly connections with others. We are all nodes in a network which is made of relationship links. These links are defined by the terms father, mother, brother, sister, son, daughter, grandfather, grandson, first cousin, uncle, aunt, friend, colleague, peer, superior, subordinate, employer, employee, neighbour, et al. We develop attachment with these affiliated individuals. We harbour passion for our parents, siblings and children. We wrongly think that they belong to us. We grieve in their grief and rejoice in their happiness. This attachment becomes the roadblock in discharging our solemn worldly duties.

That attachment is born out of ignorance becomes amply clear from considerations as aforesaid. Attachment with wealth and movable or immovable property engenders greed. Once greed settles in the human mind, honesty receives a jolt. Man becomes overly acquisitive, even justifying his immoral actions in the satisfaction of his greed. And greed does not confine itself to tangible assets like money. It also takes the form of lust for power, position and hegemony. It exists in the form of lust for gratification of various types, including sexual. Attachment weans us from the path of righteousness. This is verily the first big lesson that the Bhagwadgita has for human mortals.

Attachment engenders pain, grief and fear. Detachment liberates man. The first verse of the Bhagwadgita shows that attachment is illusory and entangles humans in the labyrinth of material world of possessions and rights. We need to take a realistic view of things, considering the eternal truths of life, death, matter, souls and the superior soul who governs the entire material world. With the eternal truths embedded in our subconscious, we shall cease to take an impassioned view of worldly objects and get over the negative states of grief and fear.

An individual human will become a realist if he always thinks that he is a spiritual entity and a temporary custodian of his material possessions. Their permanent owner is God. With this feeling constantly at the back of his mind, he will neither shy away from his duty nor will he be tormented by expectations, and will hardly fall into the states of despondency, insecurity and fear—states which are only too evident in today's life.

Chapter 2

Mental Perversion

Yadi maam pratikaaramshastram shastra panaya,
Dhartarashtra rane hanyustanmein kshemataram bhavet.

Arjun: *On the contrary, if I cease to be vindictive and drop my armoury, and in this condition if I am killed by the sons of Dhritarashtra, I shall consider myself fortunate.*

Arjun is now in a very negative mental state, far away from the core reality. When the mind is gripped by the negative emotion of attachment, reasoning takes a back seat and sense of logic is diluted. Man, in this state, ceases to differentiate between truth and untruth. His perception is dictated by emotion. He doesn't visualize reality properly.

There are numerous instances in human life when the evils of passion and attachment grip us and blind us to our solemn duties.

A few years ago, the dean of a premier management institute in India was accused of bending and bypassing the rules for facilitating the admission of his son to an MBA course. In another instance, a judge of India's Supreme Court was alleged to have helped his sons bag lucrative contracts by misusing his power and authority. In these examples, the individuals, out of attachment for their children, allegedly committed corrupt acts. They were probably blinded to their duties to uphold fairness and follow the laid down rules of propriety.

We have seen the usage of oft-repeated terms like 'stepmotherly treatment' and 'stepfatherly treatment'. Why does a person not deal with others fairly? Why and from where does an attitude of improper discrimination come? In most of such instances, persons are overwhelmed by the false feelings of belongingness. They wrongly regard relationship as physical in essence. Human relationship is really spiritual, not temporal. Human society has also been witness to parents bringing up their adopted children in a far better way than those bringing up their biological children.

How does the attitude of unfair discrimination creep in? In myriads of daily life situations, we see discriminatory behaviour. When such behaviour violates the principles of equality, it becomes improper. In corporate world, we observe subordinate employees pandering to the ego of their superiors to become their blue-eyed boys. In politics, sycophancy has probably become the master key to ascent. People who are adept in pampering the ego of their bosses are seen to rise fast. There was a very popular Internet cartoon clip showing a series of graded corporate employees lined up on a hierarchical ladder, each licking the bottom of his superior.

Human ego easily gets pampered and then becomes puffed up. Many of us possess this weakness. We develop a soft corner for the sycophant. This is mental aberration. Once we are in that situation, we become virtual slaves to our flatterer. We become oblivious to our duty and start giving the go-by to the established rules of propriety.

The second stanza of the Bhagwadgita tells us that we must continually endeavour to maintain equipoise in all life situations. Mental perversion caused by attachment will corrupt our thinking and our action in unmistakable terms. If that happens, we shall forget our true duties, and, driven by the illusory force of attachment, shall commit blunders, some of them grave.

Nothing is more unfortunate in human life than being gripped by passion and getting lost in the labyrinth of illusion. When that happens, right things appear to be wrong and facts are taken for fiction. Hence, taking a deliberate, detached perspective of things will always prevent illusory states and keep us in sync with reality.

Being overly passionate makes our personalities lopsided. We pursue our passions and, in the process, often ignore our other normal duties. Look at the many mundane situations of today's world and you will appreciate at once the veracity of this statement. A workaholic person pursues his work and is unable to devote sufficient time to his spouse and children and sends them into complaining mode. A person given to the habit of speculation gambles away his hard-earned money and lands himself and his family members in a mess. An inveterate alcoholic, a philanderer and a chain-smoker also belong to the category of persons who are slaves of passion. Passion tends to make a person immoderate and unbalanced.

Best lifestyle is one which strikes a healthy balance between work, leisure, entertainment and recreation. All work and no play makes Jack a dull boy. All play and no work will make Jack a failure. Moderation and balance are the keys to successful and happy living. In addition to the message of mental equanimity explained above, this verse of the Bhagwadgita brings home the invaluable message of observing moderation in human actions.

Chapter 3

Self-control

Klaivyam ma sma gama parth naitatwayyupapadyate,
Kshudram hridaya daurbalyam taktwottishth param tapa.

Shri Krishna: O Parth! Don't behave like an eunuch. This does not befit you at all. O valiant destroyer of enemies! Get over this frailty of the mind and stand up to perform your duty as a warrior.

The entire life is an interesting play between human mind and intellect. Many times, the intellect is unable to discern between the right and the wrong because of deficient knowledge or lack of factual clarity. It is also true that on many occasions, the intellect works properly and the person knows the right course of action but the errant mind takes him in the wrong direction. The mind, being the seat of emotions, behaves erratically while the powerful surge of emotions clouds the intellect. The person unwittingly commits blunders and gets entrapped in the fallout of those blunders.

In most of the above worldly situations, a person knows fully well what is right and what is wrong. But the overwhelming storm of emotions shakes his belief, albeit temporarily, and induces him to perform a wrong action, which goes to his detriment.

Shri Krishna, as the guide of Arjun, is not faltering in his duty of the guide. He is supposed to show Arjun the right course in the battlefield. He must guide Arjun on the way to victory in the historic battle. He is doing a perfect job of it. The human life is a battleground too. Day in and day out we are confronted with tricky matters which confuse or befuddle us. We are trapped in dilemmas or catch-22 situations. We are also swept by the surge of unfounded fear, worry or doubt and succumb to these negative emotions. In the process, we lose track of reality and start acting imprudently.

Self-control is an integral component of dharma—the divine code of righteousness expounded in *Manusmriti*, the ancient scriptural text of humanity. It occurs at two distinct levels—the physical level and the mental level. At the physical level, this control needs to be exercised in the working of our physical and cognitive senses through which we perform all our worldly tasks. Such control needs to be in accordance with the principles that promote harmony and progress.

Self-control at the mental level is no less important. We need to control the train of thoughts in the mind for alignment with the aforesaid principles. This is because of the fact that human action or karma takes effect in three modes—through the five physical sense organs (feet, genital organs, anus, hands and mouth), through the five cognitive sense organs (nose, tongue, eyes, skin and ears) and through mental thoughts.

A person without self-control is like a rudderless boat.

When we fall, we fall mostly because of lack of self-control.

The entire edifice of Jainism as a religious school is based on self-control as a practice. With this practice, one is to regulate one's senses and perform one's life karmas according to intelligent reasoning rather than dragging mental impulse.

No doubt, self-control is an immensely important key to human happiness and liberation.

In modern life, we countenance scores of situations on an everyday basis where we find the need of mind control or mental discipline. For the struggling professional working his way up the corporate ladder, for the countryside farmer tilling his land and harvesting his crop, for the judge presiding over the proceedings at the provincial high court, for the country's finance minister involved in preparing the blueprint of fiscal policy and the budget, for the businessman running an import and export trading firm, for the priest of a church or temple or mosque, or for the space scientist working in ISRO or NASA—mind control is the key to efficiency and success at work. Mind control is equally important for the housewife and that zealous individual running a charitable, social service organization. Each one needs to do his work best. Each one is expected to give his optimum output. For that, each one has to overcome the tendency towards laziness, procrastination and dishonesty. Overcoming these negative tendencies of the mind calls for mental discipline, which is exactly the message that this verse conveys.

Taking cue from the subtle message of this verse, we humans also need to be always action-oriented in life. Indolence puts us on the path of decay and decadence, leading ultimately to death, because indolence invites the devil in us to take control. In a languid existence, we give in to the forces of evil by losing self-control and walk on a regressive path. We often have the tendency to procrastinate or go easy on our defined duties. That tendency has to be curbed through willpower. Exercise of willpower and serious performance of our duties will vouchsafe happiness for us. Life will become enjoyable and fulfilling all the way.

Chapter 4

True Knowledge

Ashochyananvashochastwam pragyavadansh-cha bhashase,
Gatasunagatasunshcha nanushochanti pandita.

> Shri Krishna: *O Arjun! You are inclined to grieve over the death of those whose death should not be bemoaned. You are pretending to talk like enlightened persons. But the enlightened ones never grieve over the life or death of a human being.*

From this stanza of the Bhagwadgita comes the divine message of true knowledge. Human beings are inherently of limited knowledge and understanding. They have a grossly limited brain capacity, mental power and intellectual capability. They have, therefore, a natural tendency to believe what they understand to be the core truth, although their belief may be far removed from truth and reality. This is the fact of human life which suggests that without the light of true knowledge, we cannot progress. In many instances we remain in illusion, and in this illusionary state we indulge in wrong actions, believing them to be right. This wastes our efforts because such efforts do not bring us happiness and success. And most often we realize that we were on the wrong track only after experiencing setback and failure.

What is true knowledge? How do we define it? It is synonymous with fact and reality—reality whose perception is not limited by the power of our senses, reality whose perception is not constrained by the inherent imperfections of our intellect. The Creator of the universe is omniscient. He, who has created all sentient beings, including humans, has a clear purpose behind this creation. All sentient beings visible in their physical forms are, in essence, souls. Souls are eternal spiritual entities and continually seek fulfilment and happiness. This is their innate tendency. The Creator, or God, provides the physical body along with mind, intellect and ego to the soul to fulfil its desires. The lower order sentient beings lead a grossly corporeal existence, being endowed with inferior grades of intellect. But the human being is endowed with the highest grade of intellect. In the process of satisfying his cravings and fulfilling his desires, the human being tumbles through life, facing challenges and setbacks. But armed with true knowledge, he can overcome all challenges and attain success in his endeavours, thus gradually fulfilling all his desires. This true knowledge can only come from the all-knowing Creator.

True knowledge was imparted to human beings by God at the onset of creation in the form of Vedas. The Vedas are strands of eternal core knowledge and are divine in origin. Human beings need to fall back upon these strands of true knowledge for course correction during challenging situations of life. We can get the guidance from scriptures, preceptors or even through soul-searching in such situations. This is the divine lesson that the fourth stanza of the Bhagwadgita has for us.

True knowledge aids in fulfilling needs. It resolves problems and liberates the human being. Wrong knowledge or half knowledge may fulfil some needs but creates concomitant problems for a person and entangles him in the web of expectations and desires.

True knowledge, in the contemporary context, refers to proper techniques, processes and procedures for accomplishing a task for some desired purpose. To provide ready examples, modern surface transportation, aviation, power generation and chemical process industries are largely environmentally unfriendly and are based on half knowledge. Technologies based on true knowledge will be complete and deliver benefits without collateral harm in the form of environmental degradation, which is manifesting as serious climate change today. Medical treatment based on true knowledge of Ayurveda will not suppress symptoms of human disease through palliation, but will provide a speedy cure without any side effects. Application of true knowledge of political systems will enable nations to establish stable and durable governments that will deliver good governance. This is most relevant in the Indian context.

True knowledge of human history will unite humans, connect them with their common ancestors and help to establish global peace. It is now an open secret that history books have been tampered every now and then by unscrupulous persons. Especially in India, the former colonial rulers are accused of distorting history. British historians have written that the Aryans came to the Indian subcontinent from beyond its borders, while the fact is that the Aryans are the natives of this land and proponents of the Vedic culture. This truth has come to light now with the ongoing research on human gene structure. The term Aryan appears in the epic Mahabharat, of which the Bhagwadgita is a part. Lack of true knowledge about its history and ancestors disconnects a race with its moorings and creates an identity crisis.

True knowledge of the human soul, the superior universal

soul and their relationship will help humans to fast-track their material and spiritual progress.

With facts and reality in the form of true knowledge at the back of his mind, a person will always be in touch with the ground realities of life. With his progress path well laid out, he will not be entrapped in the state of confusion or illusion.

Chapter 5

The Mortal Body

Dehinoasmin yatha dehey kaumaram yauvanam jara,
Tatha dehantar praptirdhirarastra na muhyati.

Shri Krishna: *The soul transmigrates from one physical body to another even after the body has passed through the ageing stages of childhood, youth and senility. The soul does not change like the body throughout this process. With this understanding, persons who have wisdom and fortitude do not bemoan anyone's birth or death.*

In this stanza, Shri Krishna conveys to Arjun the fact of mortal nature of the body and the immortal nature of the soul. Actually, the human self is the soul, not the body or the mind or the intellect. And the soul is beyond ageing and death. It was never born and it will never die. It is eternal. The only change that occurs in the soul is the level of its knowledge built upon experiential understanding and the degree of its alignment with dharma.

Imagine how many blunders we make based on the mistaken notion that we are bodies and shall cease to be after death. We start saying, 'Eat, drink and be merry; there is only one life!' Our life's purpose is reduced to material gain and gratification of senses. We, individually and collectively, begin to indulge in self-aggrandizement. We hold indulgence in food, drinks, sex and wealth accumulation as the prime purpose of life. On such premises, we transgress the limits of healthy and harmonious existence and invite troubles in the form of disease, crime, fear, tension, violence and their collateral agonies.

Obsession with the mortal body increases greed and lust. With this obsession comes the urge for gratification of senses and a nagging desire for more of everything. This creates a virulent combination.

Birth, as well as death, is an event in the eternal process of life. One event is the acquisition of the physical body by the soul and the other is its relinquishment of the body. Both the events are timed by the supreme Creator, not by the soul. Whatever the supreme Creator does is in the best interests of all and perfectly justified. So, the question of grieving over this event of death should not arise at all. Whosoever views life or death in this light aligns himself with the existential reality of universe and performs karmas that promote peace, progress and prosperity. And conversely, whoever hankers after the pleasures of the body, runs, wittingly or unwittingly, into the abyss of darkness and misery.

Nothing indicates the destructible nature of the human body better than a look at a dying person. In the course of just a few moments, the person passes on from an animate state to an inanimate, lifeless state. Nothing changes in the body structurally. Only the eyes cease to see, the ears cease to hear and the heart fails to beat, bringing all bodily functions to a grinding halt. We at once begin to call that person a 'corpse'. The real person having left the body, the latter is indeed addressed correctly. The real person was the soul residing inside the body.

Only he had a name. The body is just meant to be disposed of. It has no name. It has no value. It is valued because of its owner, the soul. When the owner dwelling inside it has departed, it is reduced to a mass of rubble.

Let us always keep the stark truth of our immortal nature in our minds while working our way through the turbulent waters of the world. This will help us to navigate without fear and also without grief. We shall, then, continuously live with the realization that being eternal souls, our needs, as well as goals, are happiness and fulfilment, and these will come to us only through enlightened action. Therefore, what we really need is the nectar of truth, so that our every action is uplifting and emancipating.

In today's world, life means different things to different people. For a huge proportion of global population, life is a one-time existence. For such people who believe that we live only once, life's purpose is reduced to appeasement of senses, accumulation of wealth and pursuit of power. Gratification of senses increases indulgence and invites trouble.

Consider these. The average life expectancy has grown tremendously during the last two hundred years but so has increased the incidence of chronic disease. The average American over the age of sixty-five consumes prescription pills every day to keep going. Lifespan has increased but the quality of life has declined.

Obsession with power and hegemony has led to a race to accumulate arms among the nations of the world. This has accentuated fear. Yes, a huge chunk of global community lives in fear. The only factor that prevents a full-scale war is the horrible prospect of a nuclear holocaust. The sublime concept of immortality of the soul needs to be embraced and applied to change this horrific scenario. Immortality of the soul means that we are accountable for our actions and shall have to pay for our improper acts in the present or future life. Imbibing the concept of eternal existence of soul will generate fear of divine retribution in our minds, and this fear of retribution will refine our deeds.

Chapter 6

Dispel the Doubt

Nasato vidyatey bhavo nabhavo vidyatey sata,
Ubhayorapi drishto-antastawanyostattwa darshibhi.

Shri Krishna: *There can arise the thought in the human mind that when we are witness to death and destruction every day, then grief is natural. So, why should one not grieve? I will tell you the answer to this question.*

Human beings, being of limited knowledge and understanding, are prone to doubt and confusion. It is seen that, driven by the strong surge of emotions, a man begins to harbour doubts even over matters in which he had full clarity and conviction earlier. Undeniably, doubts do arise in the natural course of life.

World history is witness to wars, epidemics, devastating floods, ravaging earthquakes and similar calamities that have taken the tolls on millions from time to time. Daily, we observe the phenomena of numerous people being born and dying. The same is true of the lower animals. Even plants and trees are continually shrivelling and sprouting in a natural scheme of things. Yes, the bodies of living organisms are being recycled. They are formed from the basic natural elements of earth, water, fire, air and ether, and perish to return these elements to mother nature.

What is grief? It is a person's emotional reaction to an event which, in his opinion, should not have occurred or an event which has brought a trail of pain and sorrow. Grief is very natural to the ordinary persons and very unnatural to the enlightened ones who have risen above the mundane trivialities to the elevated state of spiritual existence. Such state is characterized by mental equanimity, a state in which the person sees happiness and gloom, loss and gain, grief and mirth, rise and fall, or life and death as the two sides of the same coin.

Man gets shackled by ignorance and liberated by true knowledge. The act of grieving is an expression of ignorance of the true nature of life and the process of existence. It denotes a disconnect with the stark realities of life. It is an act of childish immaturity, showing a lack of comprehension of metaphysical phenomena occurring in the universe.

Grief appears to be natural to those who are emotionally tied to the world by the bonds of attachment. Grief is natural for those with mental frailty of passion which generates the false belief of belongingness.

The message of realism—in belief and practice—is the divine message emanating from this verse. The realist understands the difference between truth and untruth because threads of existence stem only from truth, which is eternal. No object of existence can sprout from untruth. Hence, any belief or conviction based on falsity is illusory in nature. So is grief. Grieve not, because whatever has happened is for your ultimate betterment. Grieve not, because to bemoan anything is a regressive action. It wastes your time and energy with which you are supposed to continuously advance in life. Grief pulls you down in the quagmire of darkness, delusion and defeat.

Death is not an occasion to grieve but to remind ourselves of the stark reality of the soul and its divine objective.

Having the mental outlook as explained above is bound to give contemporary humans a more rational approach to life. The more rational a person is, the less superstitious he will be. And he will be a better learner and problem solver, for sure.

Consider an ace tennis player who has won three grand slams in a row and is seeded first in international rankings. He is playing in his fourth Wimbledon tournament, having won the singles title three times on previous occasions. He is expected to sail smoothly through the tournament against the opponents of lower rankings but he falters and fails. He loses his second match to an unseeded player. What happens? He is overcome by grief. But then he realizes that falling into a grievous and depression mode will make him lose his momentum for the forthcoming important tournaments. Therefore, he analyzes the cause of his failure and moves forward, putting the failure behind him. Loss of job, loss of relationship or estrangement with spouse, setback in business, etc. are some of the worldly situations that can pull a man into grief. But grief is antithetical to life, and to progress. Mental health issues, like depression, are a serious problem in the contemporary world. The way in which the tendency to grieve should be tackled is the message that emerges from this verse and this message can be a potent force in dealing with mental depression in today's life.

Having a realistic perspective on things will give today's humans a more moral and ethical edge to their interactions. The understanding that death is not an occasion to grieve will give a far more pragmatic outlook on life. It will tremendously, and comprehensively, improve the quality of our life.

Chapter 7

Soul is the Master of the Body

Antavanta ime deha nityasyokta sharirina,
Anashinoprameyasya asmadyudhyaswa bharat.

> Shri Krishna: *These bodies of flesh and bones are mortal because they sprout from ephemeral matter. The owner of every such physical body is the soul which is declared to be immortal. O Bharat, the soul is indestructible and not an object of worry. Therefore, you stop worrying about your kinsmen and engage into the war.*

In this stanza, the core philosophy of existence is expressed. The human body, or for that matter the body of any living animal or plant, is made of inert matter. This inert matter consists of the five basic elements—earth, water, fire, ether and air. From these elements are built the bodies of innumerable animals and plants inhabiting the universe. These elements belong to the inanimate matter. All material objects and living beings carved out of this matter are subject to ageing, decay and destruction.

In sharp contrast with the material objects we observe around us, the soul was never carved out or created. It exists eternally. It is not material but spiritual in constitution. It is not subject to the natural processes of decay and destruction.

It is the essence of the human being. Therefore, the death of a human being, as expressed in common parlance, should be understood as only the death of his body. The soul never dies. The body and the mind seek gratification through worldly objects but the soul seeks emancipation from misery. Its needs are different. It seeks happiness and enlightenment, which can be attained only by assiduous adherence to the principles of righteousness. If we keep this core understanding in our minds while carrying out our earthly tasks, we shall never swerve from the right path and shall never commit any blunder that may give us unhappy moments.

Whenever we humans confront a sticky situation, whenever we are in a fix and are overcome by grief, fear or worry, we need to review our situation in the light of the immanent truths of life. We need to assess our position against the metaphysical realities of the universe which reveal our true spiritual natures, our relationship with the infinite spiritual power pervading the universe and our setting in this vast material universe with kaleidoscopic variety and beauty.

Once our perspective falls in alignment with the ultimate, core truths of life, we shall most unlikely take any imprudent decision or action. We shall not give in to the surge of emotions that clouds our thinking and diverts us from the right path—the path to fulfilment, glory and bliss.

The soul is immortal, ageless and timeless. It is not made of inert matter. It is spiritual in constitution. The soul dwells inside the body. It uses this body for its onward journey in search of knowledge, fulfilment, enlightenment and freedom from bondage. It is the resident being inside the inert physical body. The body is, therefore, required to be given only as much importance as due to it under this consideration. With this understanding, a person will never grow overly materialistic and will maintain the balance between materialism and spiritualism in his life's journey.

In the business and commercial world, the very notion of the existence of soul in the human body is bound to make actions, statements and decisions of business owners more soulful and humanistic. They will be more empathetic towards their employees. They will not look at their employees as robotic working units.

In the medical world, the notion of the soul is bound to make medical practice more compassionate, which is ideally required to be in accordance with the Hippocratic Oath, under which the medical fraternity works.

In general, for the modern overly materialistic generations, the understanding of the soul is important and handy as it holds the key to the resolution of a host of problems emanating from a mad pursuit of economic growth—from the individual to the institutional level. Today, economic growth has become the cornerstone of both the individual and the institution. This has led to a lopsided development—development marked by increase of wealth in selected pockets and in a few hands—combined with concomitant erosion of mental peace. Even in the twenty-first century, 80 per cent of the global wealth is owned by less than 20 per cent of the global population. There is a stark disparity of wealth. The world probably never had so many deadly armaments which could destroy it many times over. In such a situation, the message of this verse exhorts mankind to strike a healthy balance between materialism and spiritualism.

Applying the message of this verse in our life will also make us more conscious of the quality of our actions and, accordingly, more accountable for them because of the fact that we shall continuously harbour the feeling that our immoral actions will rebound on us in this life or in the life after death.

Chapter 8

The Immortality of the Soul

*Ya ainam vetti hantaram yashchayinam manyatey hatam,
Ubhau tau na vijaneeto nayam hanti na hanyate.*

Shri Krishna: *Anyone who thinks that the soul is killed or can be killed is not aware of the reality. The reality of the soul is its immortal nature.*

This stanza is in further explanation of the previous one. Most of us think that the human being ceases to exist with his death because we do not realize that the essence of the human being is not the body or the mind or the sensory organs, but the invisible, infinitesimal soul. The body of flesh, fat, blood and bones is a multi-sheathed abode of the soul. It is destructible, while the soul lives on.

Just because we do not see the soul does not mean that we should discount or dismiss its existence. In fact, any sentient being is a soul. Any animate entity is spiritual in essence. The soul is not made of raw elements of mother nature. It is, therefore, not subject to the laws of material universe. It cannot be cut or burnt. It has no shape. The body remains sentient or live as long as the soul resides in it. The moment the soul exits the body, the latter becomes dead. It begins to rot and decay and dissolve in the soil.

The soul is recognized by its innate characteristics and tendencies which include its immaterial nature, formlessness, agelessness, immortality, desire, love, hatred, jealousy and passion. Some of these characteristics are in common with the universal soul controlling everything, whom we call paramatma (supreme soul) or God. The human soul is inherently a seeker of bliss. For this, it is engaged in a continuous process of refinement based on experiential knowledge. This knowledge is acquired through multiple experiences of life which occur according to the principle of cause and effect. These experiences include episodes of pain and pleasure, happiness and gloom or success and failure, all of which validate the divine principle of cause and effect permeating the universe.

The soul is pious, not evil, but its knowledge and understanding of things is grossly incomplete. A person commits evil acts out of gross ignorance because his essence—the soul—is swayed by the improper tendencies of the mind and imperfections of the intellect.

Many contemporary schools of human thought do not subscribe to the belief in the existence of a soul. They talk of body, mind and intellect and the interplay of these entities. But the existence of the soul is as obvious as the existence of the sun, moon, stars, wind and water. The soul is an animate element in a living organism and this understanding is intrinsic to the working and behaviour of all living beings inhabiting this vast universe.

The verse brings out a great message—that the soul is nothing external to you; it is just you. It seeks pleasure and happiness and abhors pain and sorrow. It is rational in outlook and a seeker of truth. It inherently seeks freedom from bondage.

It learns from experiences of others as well as its own sweet and sour experiences. It nurtures desires and makes efforts to fulfil them. All that the soul or you desire is achievable through right knowledge and its application.

Belief in the existence and immortality of the soul will align the modern man with the true objective of human existence. Instead of saying, 'Eat drink and be merry; you live only once,' he will say, 'Accumulate virtue; you need happiness and liberation.' This belief will dramatically transform human perspective on life. It will make a person less materialistic and far more balanced, as he will be aligned with the core reality. It will bring a great attitudinal change. If human attitude changes for the better, everything else changes for the better too.

If I am clear and sure that I have to embark on a new life after death—life in which I shall have a new body, a new set of parents, a new home and locations and an entirely new set of circumstances, leaving behind all past life assets, possessions and even memories—I would start viewing life quite differently. I would realize fast that what I seek is bliss and I need to work for bliss. I need to work for bringing smiles on the faces of other humans, for striking the notes of harmony in my own small world, for preserving the purity of the physical environment, for making the flowers of spring bloom all over. I need to work with all my might to make the world a happier and more peaceful place.

As mentioned above, the firm belief that human beings are eternal spiritual entities is bound to make us humane and moral. Hence, adaptation of the eternal truth of immortality of the soul in our lives will be a huge factor in our moral transformation and, as a result, in bringing down the incidence of crime and corruption in the civilized world.

Chapter 9

Duty is Religion

Swadharma mapi chavekshya na vikampitu marhasi,
Dharmyaddhi yuddhachheyo anyat kshatriyasya na vidyatey.

Shri Krishna: *You consider yourself as a righteous and religious person. That is all the more reason for you not to run away from this battle. For a Kshatriya, nothing is more rewarding than the observance of his duty as a warrior, which needs to be performed religiously.*

Religion is duty and duty is religion. Duty is the set of actions that we are called upon to perform in roles that obligate us to fulfil our responsibilities for maintaining peace, progress and prosperity in the society and for ensuring stability and harmony around us. If we perform our duty religiously, we are conducting ourselves righteously. If we are devoted to our duty, we are devoted to God. Work is worship. The work of an engineer or a physician or a trader or a soldier is distinctive and unique in its own way and calls for a devoted performance. This devoted performance of vocational roles is the most important element of religiosity. Other things come later, because by performing our assigned roles in the society well, we are already doing a major justice to the living beings around us.

A Kshatriya's solemn duty is to decimate the enemy of his motherland. Nothing should take precedence over this prime duty. Duty well performed is equivalent to worshipping the Almighty. Hence, your duty should mean almost everything to you. Human duty has two broad dimensions. One is the set of tasks that a person performs for earning his livelihood. The other is the set of tasks that he is required to perform as a responsible citizen of his country and as member of his own community and family. In both qualitative and quantitative terms, these tasks should extend the maximum benefit to others, thereby promoting their welfare continuously.

Whenever you experience a surge of emotions that suggests you a certain course of action or inaction which is not in accordance with your duty, you should consider yourself on the wrong track. Doing so will immediately help you realize that you need course correction. Thus, the litmus test of appropriateness of your contemplated action is whether the same is going to be conducive to peace, harmony and welfare of all and whether it is going to uphold the values of dharma.

A warrior's duty is to fight against the enemies of fairness and justice. Fighting will undoubtedly involve bloodshed, but this bloodshed is definitely for a noble and well-meaning cause. Every member of the human society has his own set of duties to perform and these duties constitute his role. A role well performed is like an oblation or offering to God. Shying away from duty is ignoring the injunction of the supreme Creator. This needs to be borne in mind by every person. Duty well performed takes us nearer to God. Hence, continuously cultivate the sense of duty and diligently perform your defined role in the society. Nothing is more important than this.

Modern human society has been witness to wide discussions

for upholding and protection of human rights. Mahatma Gandhi had said that human duties were more important than human rights, because in the performance of human duties, human rights were automatically protected.

In today's scenario, as mentioned above, duty consciousness has been overwhelmed by rights consciousness. Everywhere, we witness shrill cries for protection of individual rights. Institutions like UNHRC and national and international courts are vigorously pursuing the agendas of protection of human rights all over. At the individual level, people are observed to be more demanding for what they feel is their due.

We all need to stress on developing our sense of duty.

Whatever be one's role in the society—that of a student, teacher, employee, employer, workplace superior, workplace subordinate, parent, child, sibling, etc.—one should focus on the proper discharge of his duty. A student needs to observe regularity in attending academic sessions and performing home assignments. He ought to respect his teachers and guides. The teacher's focus should be on developing interest and passion among his students and helping them achieve their desired grades. Activities which digress from this duty, like students indulging in campus politics, are not aligned with this philosophy.

An employee should focus on giving his very best at his job and achieving the set targets. He should not think about what he deserved or what he got in the form of salary or annual increments vis-à-vis his peers. The employer's focus should be on getting the best out of his employees through motivation without exploiting them for his profits. A workplace superior should work towards development of his subordinates and the subordinate towards satisfying his superior. A physician should work with compassion and try to cure his patients in minimum time rather than prolong the treatment driven by monetary greed. In a democratic country, politicians should focus on public welfare agenda and not on placation of specific sections of voter community. The citizens should focus on what they can do for their country rather than what their country gives them.

The entire focus of human activities needs to be built strongly on assiduous performance of duties. In formal settings, the duties are defined and documented. In other situations, the duties are informally known and understood.

Focus on performance of duty will usher in changes in the society for its betterment and make the world a truly better place to live in.

Chapter 10

The Twin Benefits of Duty

Nato va prapsyasi swargam jitwa va bhokshyasey mahim,
Tasmaduttishtha kauteya yuddhaya kritinishchaya.

Shri Krishna: *If you get killed in the battle, you will be rewarded with paradise and if you are victorious in the battle, you will rule the earth. Therefore, realize the twin benefits of performing your present duty and get determined to discharge your warrior's duty in this battle.*

Duty delivers a man. Duty refines him comprehensively. Duty is the gateway to happiness, success and salvation. Therefore, a human being should never shirk his duty. While performing his duty, a person should never ponder or worry much over the consequences of his actions. These consequences are beyond his control and belong to the realm of the higher power that rules the universe. The results of human actions are equal and opposite to those actions in the sense that they follow the immanent law of cause and effect that regulates the entire universe. Virtuous actions in the nature of assiduous performance of duty unmistakably bring boons and rewards and vicious actions in the nature of duty dereliction attract punishment. The law of cause and effect is administered by the Almighty and is inviolable, because it maintains perfect justice in the universe inhabited by sentient beings.

We all have defined duty and responsibility towards our employers, customers, clients, governments, communities, families, nations and the world at large. It is expected of us that we correctly understand our roles and perform those roles properly. We may not be short-term gainers materially in the course of this performance; we may even undergo suffering and loss, but in the long term we shall be more than compensated and adequately rewarded for our actions. This divine message is conveyed through Shri Krishna's sermon.

Duty has to be understood as distinct from rights. As mentioned before, these days we hear lots of shrill cries over human rights. But nobody talks of duties. Duties are actions but rights can be likened to rewards which actually belong to God's domain. Duties are actions in full control of human beings and so, quite naturally, humans are expected to discharge those duties. If human duties are well performed, religiosity is at once observed. Therefore, it is important to perform human duties assiduously. Duty is service, right is remuneration. Duty is charity, right is reward. Duty is struggle against injustice, right is justice. Duty brings twin rewards—of material nature and of sublime, spiritual nature.

The past or contemporary world is witness to erosion of peace and harmony due to the dilution of sense of duty by humans. When a human tendency for seizing and wresting things replaces a tendency for serving and giving, problems set in. Litigation, wars and acrimonious discussions are indicators of humans abdicating their sense of duty.

Performance of duty in thought and action builds good human beings. The sense of duty defines human character. The term duty is comprehensive, covering moral, ethical and legal aspects of human action. Hence, a dutiful person is a righteous and progressive person.

The message underlying this divine verse tells mankind of the tremendous payoffs of observing duty. If a person is focused on performing his duties well, he is leading a good life. Success is sweet but failure is a bitter potion that grooms a person for the next sweet success. But for attaining success, a person needs to work hard and become more efficient and productive. He needs to work with honesty and transparency too. Duty includes these and many other aspects of life. Practical sense of humanistic duty will make a person humble and compassionate. He will respect others and will get respect in return. He will be generous and liberal, far removed from the sectarian zealots and religious fanatics witnessed even today. His heightened sense of duty will improve him as a person thoroughly.

Developing a perspective of being more dutiful will deliver better parents at home and better teachers at school. It will build better policemen and better politicians. It will create more sporting sportspersons and more productive professionals.

Contemporary humans are wasting a lot of time, money and energy in preservation of rights. Application of the message of this verse can bring about a paradigm shift in their focus and perspective. With such perspective in position, global peace would no longer remain a distant dream.

In modern times, developing the sense of duty by civilized humans will develop their character. Imagine the tremendous amount of time and money that is spent in litigation all over the world. Development of the sense of duty will reduce this in a big way. At the individual level, being more dutiful will make a person more understanding, accommodative, adjustable and empathetic. It will reduce stress like nothing else can, making man far more calm and contented. At the macro level, it will make human institutions—political, economic, social or legal—more responsive as well as objective, bringing greater equity and justice in their operations.

Chapter 11

The Eternal Law of Karma

Karmanyevadhikarastey ma phaleshu kadachana,
Ma karmaphal heturbhurma te sango astvakarmani.

Shri Krishna: *You possess the right to perform your karmas but not to the rewards of those karmas. Do your karma as a duty without fixing sight on the reward. You should also shun indolence and continuously engage in proper, useful, productive karmas.*

The eternal law of karma brings out the core philosophy of existence. It shows that performance of duty is the essence of successful living. The action of performing the duty belongs to the realm of the humans but the bestowal of reward belongs to the realm of the Creator, who rewards His human subjects for their dutiful actions in a fair manner. He maintains perfect justice in His universe by this fair bestowal of rewards. So, man must not be anxious about the results of his actions. His obsession with the result or reward will interfere with the performance of action itself.

Karma with attachment to rewards binds a person, and unattached karma liberates him. The doctrine of karma is the supreme spiritual law of cause and effect operating in the universe with mathematical precision. The performer of the karma does not understand which karma will yield which result and in how much time. This is something beyond the comprehension of mortals and rightly so. This is because knowledge of future events in fructification of past karmas will hinder the evolution of the human soul.

The law of karma is immanent and is inevitably and instantly called into play on human action. It is an intrinsic and inbuilt operational law and works in a dynamic mode. Therefore, this law is also likened to the creator God by some schools of religion. Buddhism and Jainism do not have the concept of God or soul. But Buddhism and Jainism do believe in the dynamic principle of cause and effect and, therefore, indirectly subscribe to the idea that a dynamic power operates in the universe that maintains perfect justice in it. To maintain this justice, it has to continuously grant reward or punishment to human beings for their virtuous or vicious deeds, respectively. But in what manner, how and when these rewards or punishments will be meted out to human subjects cannot and should not be known to these subjects.

The world of human mortals is a big kingdom administered by the almighty Creator. He administers this kingdom perfectly. Complete justice is meted out to each individual against his action. Incomplete or improper justice delivered by the human courts is redeemed by Him. The law of karmic retribution makes that happen.

The human life, therefore, is a saga of karmas. Do your best dutiful karma and then forget about its result. If you start worrying about the result before the karma, you will be unable to perform that karma properly and if you begin to worry about the result after the performance of karma, you will not be able to maintain the mental peace and posture to embark on a new set of life-elevating karmas. We are all driven by the urge to do karmas and are, at the same time, also driven by the effects of karmas performed in the past. Both sets of karmas determine our future. Hence, karmas drive our life and determine the events of life, whether good or bad. Life is an eternal narrative of karmas.

In modern-life situations, there is lot of talk on productivity and efficiency improvement. Hundreds of workshops and training sessions run on the subject. The focus appears to be more on the systems of working. From the systems, the focus needs to shift partially to the attitude of working. If this is done, we will get an exponential increase in productivity without too much application of technological implements, like computing devices and speciality software.

In today's life, we are obsessed with results and rewards of our actions, as mentioned earlier. People are exhorted to be result-oriented in the corporate world. This verse tells us to be action-oriented rather than result-oriented. Being action-oriented will bring us better, bigger and faster results and rewards. At the same time, the absence of expectation will prevent dejection and disappointment. An individual can test the veracity of this statement by experimenting just for one day. Let him fix up a day on which he determinedly remains action-oriented. He makes perfect use of his time and spends a neat, balanced, productive twenty-four hours. Then let him compare the day with the previous days. He will find that the day was spent in a happy, satisfied and ebullient mood. He will have discovered the ideal way to live.

Chapter 12

Mental Fortitude, Intellectual Clarity

Siddhayasiddhayo samo bhutwa samatwam yoga uchyatey,
Shrutivipratipanna tey yada sthasyati nishchala,
Samadhavachala buddhistada yogamavapsyasi.

Shri Krishna: *Maintaining an even keel in happiness and sorrow, in success as well as failure is the hallmark of yoga. When you steer clear of confusion caused by messages of shrutis[*] and your intellect becomes balanced and composed, you will attain this yoga state.*

Getting entangled in the expectation of fruits of actions is not the progressive way forward for humans. When you have learned to view loss and gain alike, success and failure alike and happiness and misery alike, you are really on the way to developing mental equanimity. This is the yoga of fortitude that elevates humans to the next level—spiritually. This is the yoga which establishes a mental framework in which a person will never fail to see reason and never fail to act in accordance with reason. This is the yoga of enlightened intellect.

---

*Orally transmitted scriptures

When you do not feel elevated in success or depressed in failure, you are in a state of yoga that harbours a balanced intellect. You become emotionally detached to such contrasting states. Once your emotional fixation with success and failure is broken, you enter into the realm of freedom which enables you to perform every karma in accordance with enlightened reason. Such karma will never fail you. It will bring you material bounties, mental peace and spiritual succour.

There are scriptures, and derived scriptures, by the dozens in the world. A human being is endowed with limited intellectual capacity which restricts his understanding and application of tenets enshrined in the scriptures. Reading too many scriptural texts often leads to confusion, and as a result of this, the person is unable to exercise his innate sense of logic and reasoning. He falls prey to poor decision-making and suffers its baneful consequences.

Happiness and sorrow are to be considered as mere reactions to human situations. Situation per se is neither good nor bad. It is the outcome of a person's past qualitative actions. Hence, in spiritual terms, every situation that a person faces is for his spiritual progress. To get over the mental fixation of the good-bad, low-high, profit-loss, success-failure and similar stereotypes, one needs to develop one's mental fortitude, which, as mentioned earlier, is the sign of yoga.

Persons having mental fortitude maintain their balance of mind in all situations—low or high. It will not be difficult to locate such people; you will find many of them in your communities. You will also observe that these people are happy and successful. Mundane success is the ladder to spiritual salvation.

Mental fortitude is the touchstone of spiritual refinement. Its presence in a person indicates a dispassionate outlook and a heightened sense of objectivity. It is the prime armament with which to counter the evil forces that grip a man's mind and stall his material and spiritual progress.

Modern-day human beings need to develop mental equanimity more than anything else. The entire generation is overly materialistic. Our spiritual quotient is low and materialistic quotient is high. Many of us tend to exult over success and wail over failure. We hardly realize that either situation is abnormal, because in both situations we are thrown out of gear. In each situation, we lose grip over ourselves and start thinking irrationally.

The matter of orally transmitted scriptures has been referred to in this verse of the Bhagwadgita. Human life has been witness to the confusion caused by deliberate or ignorant misinterpretation of scriptures. The present world is home to several mainstream religions and their numerous variants. There are dozens of scriptures and dozens of explanations and interpretations of each scripture. Many of these interpretations have shades of differences. Such differences create utter confusion in the minds of average human beings who follow these scriptures with faith. Core truths sometimes suffer casualty and half-truths come to occupy the mental space of people. This is most unfortunate.

Modern man has an option. He can steer clear of the varying shades of scriptural interpretations and focus on developing his mental fortitude. That is an easier and more practical way of going forward, and can be the simplest solution to the set of complex problems created by the vast multiplicity of ideologies.

The great teaching of this verse, if applied in modern-life situations, will give us a sharp hedge against failure and disappointment in life. It will groom us for material success and spiritual salvation.

Chapter 13

Composed Intellect

Prajahaati yada kaamaan sarvaan parth manogataan,
Aatmanyevatmana tushta stithpragyast dochyatey.

Shri Krishna: O Parth! When a person relinquishes all desires and becomes self-contented, he comes to possess a composed intellect.

Desires agitate the mind and a mind in a state of agitation adversely affects the intellect. It clouds and blurs the intellect. It leads to confusion and loss of clarity. Desires generate the mental states of passion, anger, greed and pride which overpower the intellect, thus making it ineffective and incapable of guiding the human being. The profound effect of desires makes a person restless and ill at ease. Consequently, he loses control of his own self and starts committing blunders.

Contentment establishes inner peace, and a peaceful state of the mind lends composure to the intellect, thus making it capable of working objectively and rationally. The intellect then becomes not only sharp, but powerful enough to reign in the reckless mind. A powerful intellect holding sway over the mind is the sure passport to human success and happiness.

It may be noted in the above context that neither the mind nor the intellect is animate. Both are inert material entities. They are powered by the immortal soul. Therefore, the soul or the self has to understand the difference between the mind and the intellect and their respective roles in human life. Both the mind and the intellect are tools available to the soul for understanding, thought and action. A powerful, pure intellect can control the errant and excitable mind for following the right course of action.

A composed intellect is that which is not vitiated by the impurities of material nature. Through the working of such an intellect, a person is able to exercise reason and judgement well. He is able to differentiate between the good and the bad, between the beneficial and the harmful, between illusion and reality. He works through enlightened reason and his approach is fully rational. Such a person is not controlled by the excitable mind but he controls that mind.

If Hitler had had a composed intellect, he would not have carried out the holocaust.

If Mussolini had had a composed intellect, he would not have created the cult of fascism.

It is easy to see that in modern-life situations, it is only the high intensity desires that vitiate the mind and blur the intellect. We often see judgemental behaviour on the part of individuals in certain institutions and then those individuals paying heavily for it. In the past, a famous and talented cricketer in India had called the cricket test team selectors a 'bunch of jokers' when they did not select him in the national team for a test series. As a result, he was never again selected for any other matches.

We see many such examples. A Cabinet minister publicly criticizes the prime minister for his policy pronouncements. And in a few days, he is eased out of the Cabinet. An employee is vociferous about the unprofessional working of his employer company. He doesn't last long in the company as he is soon shown the exit door. In all these cases, individuals overwhelmed by anger and frustration allow the surge of emotions to swamp the intellect.

The intellect makes the individual behave in an irrational manner to his own serious disadvantage. Being judgemental means that you are venting out your irritation and frustration on others by criticizing their nature, behaviour or actions. Instead of being overly critical and judgemental, we should focus on what we can do best in the nature of useful contributions to the institutions we belong to. Therefore, we must try to maintain the composure of the intellect.

In modern-life situations, time is at a premium. With the ubiquitous mobile phone in our hands or pockets every moment, we are always in a hurry, in some expectation, in a state of anxiety and, above everything else, overly ambitious. We feel that we are highly empowered—carrying moments of time in our hands. That keeps us on the drive, always trying to push things. Is our intellect calm and composed all through this?

We must find time to relax. We must slow down. Life is too precious to chase wealth continuously. We do not stop chasing it even when we have gone to sleep. We keep the mobile phone right beside our bed.

We find time to relax, to enjoy the beauty and bounty of nature by visiting virgin beaches, invigorating hilly locales and glistening grassy green lands during planned vacation periods and even there we carry our mobile sets with us—to remain 'connected'.

We are all undermining our intellectual composure.

A composed intellect steers the life boat of a person in the right direction by providing guidance to the soul on the basis of righteousness and reason. The quality of intellect is the key to the quality of human karma and the latter holds the key to human happiness. A composed intellect is balanced—always open to accretion of knowledge and correction of wrong ideas and notions. Such an intellect is the cornerstone of the comprehensive progress of man.

Chapter 14

Stability of the Intellect

Dukheshwanu dwignamana sukheshu vigatspriha,
Veetraag bhaya krodha sthit dhirmu niruchyatey.

Shri Krishna: *A person who does not grieve in adversity nor rejoices in favourable situations, a person who has relinquished or overcome passion, fear and anger, such a person possesses stability of the intellect.*

This is in elaboration and explanation of what was expressed in the previous chapter. It needs a powerful posture of detachment to develop equanimity of mind which leads to a condition in which a person does not grieve over adverse situations and also does not rejoice in happy and favourable situations. Such a person is one who has got over the cardinal negative tendencies of passion, fear and anger. Such a person has intellectual stability and composure. He is then said to be in a spiritually elevated state.

When a person discovers contentment in his heart and continually engages in actions promoting the welfare of fellow beings and actions that are in line with the divine commandments of his Creator and Master, he doesn't get agitated by others' reactions to his actions and maintains inner peace. He is, then, not passionately attached to material riches and, therefore, he rises above anger. He is, in such a state, regarded as intellectually well-postured and aligned with the supreme divinity.

Strong cravings and desires will not agitate the mind of a person who is evenly disposed to loss and gain, to pleasure and pain, to reward and punishment and to prosperity and penury.

A stable intellect enables a person to think rationally and analyze situations logically. He remains grounded in reality and does not fall prey to delusion. He is well on track as far as spiritual growth is concerned.

Developing stability of the intellect is also an exercise of the mind. The mind has to be controlled and disciplined so that it does not give way to surges of fear, grief or worry. It also has to overcome passion. A mind which is free from such baneful elements is pliable and amenable to control by the intellect, and that is the ideal situation for a human being to be in.

'To be free is not merely to cast off one's chains, but to live in a way that respects and enhances the freedom of others,' said Dr Nelson Mandela, a man whose life exemplified fearlessness and mental composure.

Anger is delusionary. So is arrogance. If I shout at my peer for being silly, I am deluding myself and disrespecting his freedom. If I start slandering less wealthy or less endowed people out of arrogance, I am again deluding myself and impeding my spiritual growth. A stable intellect is not something that many persons possess in contemporary world. To overcome passion, fear and anger is no mean task. But the mere understanding that a stable intellect is the passport to freedom and success in this fast-paced life is important for the average individual.

The intellect in man is more important than his mind. If the enlightened intellect bridles the mind and keeps it under control, man can never falter in his actions. He can never swerve from the right path. That underscores the need to keep the intellect stable and in command of the ever-excitable mind.

Modern psychologists use a term called emotional quotient. This term connotes the emotional maturity of a person, i.e. the degree to which that person acts by reason rather than emotion. The message of this beautiful verse, if applied in a person's life, will enhance his emotional quotient.

Anger is natural. Irritability is natural. Fear is natural and so is worry. But these natural human states undermine man's productivity, success and happiness. So the key is to rise above these negative states of the mind. The key is the application of the intellect which holds control of the deviant mind. An intellect well in control of the mind remains stable and guides you well, whereas an intellect not in control of the mind is dragged by the mind itself into zones of perversity and instability where negativities of all sorts find a fertile ground for growth.

A stable intellect is unaffected by the raging emotional storms. Such storms are often so heavy and powerful that they vitiate the intellectual faculty which ceases to function in the normal manner. This is a very damaging state to be in. This state makes a human being prone to error and, more than that, delusion. And committing a mistake without being aware of it can be most detrimental. That underlines the importance of this verse.

Chapter 15

The Demise of Desire

Vishaya vinivartantey niraharasya dehina,
Rasvarja raso apyasya param drishtava nivartatey.

Shri Krishna: *A person who is deprived of food, drinks and other articles of physical gratification beyond his needs, ceases to partake them but his cravings for them don't die. In his mind, he continues to long and crave for these articles of enjoyment. But when he comes in alignment with the Creator, his flaming desires based on greed are extinguished.*

There is a clear and subtle difference between need and greed. Eatables are required by a human being for survival. But overindulgence in food and drinks for gratification of taste buds is a passionate action born out of desire. This is contrary to righteousness. This is antithetical to spirituality. Spirituality, by its core definition, is a course of action in sync with the divine laws of existence set by the Creator.

Desires exist in various shades and colours. A person needs two pairs of footwear and perhaps five pairs of garments for his day-to-day requirements. But if he wants to live in exquisite style or wishes to flaunt his enormous wealth, he will fill his wardrobe with a hundred items of clothing and fifty pairs of footwear. Human desire is fed and fuelled by greed. This desire is not diminished by its fulfilment but only increases further. The flames of desire find further fuel in fulfilment. Ultimately, these flames start consuming the person who harbours the desires.

So, desires need to be curbed. Noble and altruistic desires do not fall in this category as they are not engendered by greed. Desires create in a person such a strong urge to accumulate and enjoy that he transgresses the limits of moderation, and thereby invites troubles for himself. Desires emanating from passion and greed land you in a labyrinth of delusion and wrongdoing, and the inevitable result of that is suffering.

The death knell of desire can be sounded only by acquisition of true knowledge and based on that, by treading the path of virtuosity and moderation. True knowledge is not the exclusive domain of uniquely positioned scholars and saints. It is available to common folks through the signs and signals of mother nature, through the constantly palpable inner voice of the supreme Creator which guides His human subjects for their happiness, welfare and salvation.

Moderation is the important key to control greed and desire. Moderation is demonstrated by nature in its everyday operations. The ever-benevolent nature takes tender care of all living beings. The sun with its warmth and light, the life-sustaining wind and the bountifully flowing rivers provide their elements to humans and other beings with controlled intensity. If the sun began to shine brighter and hotter and the wind turned into a blizzard and the rivers began to swell and overflow, entire life on earth would be devastated. Immoderately hot sun would scorch humans out of existence. High winds and storms would also produce disastrous effects. Hence the basic elements of nature and the celestial bodies work in controlled limits set forth by the supreme Creator and Sustainer. He has infused discipline and moderation in the flow of his primordial elements. Man needs to understand that in order to remain in harmony with nature, he too needs to become like nature—moderate and disciplined.

Desires elevate a man but also depress him. It depends upon how he goes about fulfilling them. It is related to the quality of his karmas in the pursuit of the desired goals. Material desires, like acquisition of wealth, position or power, can be fulfilled by righteous means and also by employing wrongful means. In the former case, fulfilment of desires by a person brings about a qualitative change in him—for the better. But material success achieved through questionable means pulls down the achiever in spiritual terms. In either case, a mindless pursuit of material goals distances a person from God. His flaming desires are snuffed when he begins to align himself with the immanent laws set in by the almighty Creator.

Desires bind a person to the rigmarole of mundane life. When he attunes himself with the Creator dwelling inside and becomes a yogi, the fog of his intellect clears and his flaming desires springing from passion and greed are doused.

In today's life, many of the problems of human beings emanate from greed and desire based thereon. The commercial world of business is constantly on the move to spur human consumption and spending. We see advertisements on cars, colas and chocolates doing exactly this. The ubiquitous mobile handset was possessed by less than 1 per cent of the population just about twenty years ago. Today, a large majority of persons possesses it and also quickly discards the old one, replacing it with a newer model.

Modern man needs to tone down his proclivity for self-aggrandizement. He needs to curb his hedonistic tendency.

Moderation in living is the big lesson that this verse of the Bhagwadgita offers us. The moment we cross the limits of moderation, we violate the laws of nature and invite trouble. Healthy ambition, which promotes competition and efficiency in our institutions, is good, but ambition based on greed is never good.

Chapter 16

Perspective of a Yogi

Ya nisha sarvabhutanaam tasyaam jaagrati sanyami,
Yasyaam jaagrati bhutani sa nisha pashyato muney.

Shri Krishna: *Ordinary people and yogis have different perspectives on life and look at worldly matters in contrasting ways. Matters in which ordinary folks are casual and careless alert the yogis and make them serious and focused. Similarly, mundane matters which are important for ordinary persons receive passing attention from yogis. Such matters, which usually pertain to wealth, fame, position or power are trivialized by the yogis.*

Materialistic issues do not excite the yogi or create passionate desires in him. On the contrary, his passion for truth and spiritual elevation constantly grows. His passion for experiencing divinity is continuously at work to refine him. Ordinary persons are always steeped in desires for accumulating wealth and increasing other material possessions. They are not inclined towards spirituality or the subtle truths of life that will elevate them to higher planes of existence.

Ordinary people lead ordinary lives. Most of them remain

engrossed in daily issues of bread and butter, in the daily chores attached with their domestic and professional spheres and in realizing their ambitions. They are too involved with worldly matters to look beyond the temporal. They lack the spiritual perspective on life, although spirituality constitutes the core of life. A yogi, on the other hand, even if leading the life of an ordinary householder, attends to all his worldly duties, without getting overly involved or obsessed. He realizes that human beings are essentially spiritual entities who seek happiness and fulfilment. Material possessions give temporary happiness and do not provide lasting fulfilment. Lasting fulfilment comes when the raging flames of desire have been extinguished and that happens through gradual tuning with the supreme spiritual entity of the universe.

The perspective of a yogi on life is, therefore, sublime and spiritual. He understands the true purpose of living and seeks to fulfil that purpose through an approach which is central and balanced. He realizes that a soul keeps on struggling through life after life till it has fully embraced the tenets of righteousness or dharma. Once that happens, it is liberated from the cycle of births and rebirths. It attains moksha.

The yogi is not a recluse. He can remain in the thick of worldly life and yet can pursue the spiritual objective. The world is effectively the training and development centre for the human soul. The institutions of human living—family, government, business and professional organizations, nation and the global 'village'—are intended to provide the necessary working platforms for this training and development of the individual.

The modern man needs to realize what is more important for him and what is less important. Is appeasement of taste buds important or satiation of hunger? Is money more important than the means of earning it or is it the other way round? Is knowledge more important than learning? Is truthfulness more important than tactfulness? Is it more important for the body to be clean or to be attractive externally? Are dedicated efforts important or is success? Is action for public welfare more important than the fame which follows it? In marriage, is love more important or sex? The answers to all these questions should be clear to the modern human being for his happiness and welfare. If he has the answers and patterns his lifestyle on these answers, he will tread the path of a yogi and will constantly progress in life—not just materially but also spiritually.

The very fact that man is a spiritual being indicates that he needs to maintain a balance between materialism and spiritualism in his life journey. Being overly materialistic will never pay, not even materially. Being overly materialistic will never bring happiness and peace. This fact has been tested many times over. The life and attitude of a yogi is the model for education and also for gradual emulation.

Human life has been granted by the Creator to make the eternal soul refined through karma. Elevating karmas refine the soul. This refinement is in the nature of growing proclivity of the soul for action in line with dharma or righteousness. The tendency of the soul for righteous action develops swiftly through communion with the Creator and this is exactly the message that this verse conveys. Drawing from this message, contemporary humans should give up the obsession for money, fame, status or power. They need to understand that the world is the platform for their refinement and improvement. With this perspective, their attitudes and actions would approach that of the yogis. They will enhance harmony and happiness.

Chapter 17

The Virtues of Yagya

Devaan bhavayatanen te deva bhavayantu va,
Parasparam bhavayanta shreya param vapsyath.

Shri Krishna: *Appeasing devatas through yagya will make them shower their blessings on you. The practice of yagya will enable you to continuously receive rewards from the devatas whom you have placated, and through this process you will obtain the ultimate benefits of life.*

Devatas are the entities that bestow material benefits on human beings. The five elemental devatas—prithvi (earth), jal (water), agni (fire), aakash (ether) and vayu (air)—bestow these benefits to the yagya performer many times over when they are purified and nourished through agnihotra yagya. Living entities who provide benefits to human beings through this give-and-take process also fall in the category of devatas. The greatest devata is the supreme Creator who administers this vast universe and maintains perfect justice in it.

Any activity which is collective, contributory, participatory, and brings benefits to all participants is yagya. On this planet earth, every business activity is a yagya. The work of every government, and hence every political functionary, is a yagya. The research work performed by every scientist is a yagya. The farmer who cultivates crops on his fields is also performing yagya as he is going to feed thousands of persons through his produce. A teacher who imparts moral and professional education to students also acts as a yagya performer because his training is going to make the students worthy and useful members of the society. A person entering into married life is undertaking a yagya too. In the civilized world, at any moment of time, countless yagyas are going on, with all participants deriving tangible or intangible benefits out of them.

Human engagement in useful and constructive activity is a yagya. Worship of the Creator is also a yagya as it refines the worshipper and improves the quality of his actions or karmas. Better karmas enhance the peace and happiness of others while interacting with the worshipper. Dissemination of true knowledge based on divine scriptures is also a yagya, as knowledge serves as the fundamental tool for noble actions and their beneficial effects.

Human development happens through actions that belong to the process of yagya. Whatever a man seeks or aspires for can be acquired through religious performance of such actions. When a man has satisfied all his wants and mundane desires, he seeks salvation, for which, again, yagya serves as the vehicle.

In view of the above explanation, a subtle understanding of the nature and significance of yagya is greatly important for a person. With this understanding in his mind, he will consciously remain in action to further the life interests of others and his own.

Modern man is not appeasing the devatas, but doing just the opposite of that. He is continuously polluting the air on the planet through harmful industrial pollutants. Huge amounts of garbage is being dumped into rivers and oceans on a daily basis. This has already started bringing calamitous effects in the form of tsunamis, wildfires, floods and extreme climatic conditions. This verse advises us to be gentle and friendly towards nature and not ravage it like we have been doing for a long time. It gives us the great message of making our activities, procedures and processes environment-friendly. By doing so, we can maintain stability and harmony among the elements of nature and prevent disastrous conditions.

Agnihotra yagya is a great depolluting measure and is a potent solution to the problem of air pollution that has become so acute today. One gram of cow's ghee administered to the sacrificial fire of agnihotra yagya generates one tonne of pure oxygen. One tonne of oxygen is a great amount of life-giving and life-supporting element. This can nurture and nourish numerous plants, animals and humans. Modern man should scientifically analyse the effects of agnihotra yagya on the atmosphere. He needs to practise this yagya for deriving the multiple benefits that it carries.

To convince the sceptics about the benefits of agnihotra yagya, it may be stated that this yagya involves appeasement of the five elemental devatas. Everything in this world is made up of some or the other combination of these five elements existing as water, earth, fire, air and ether. Mollification of these primal elements through the technique of agnihotra yagya makes the benefits flow to you at the subtle levels of nanotechnology. Nature becomes very powerful at those levels. This can be understood from the scientific fact that a few grams of nuclear fuel are sufficient to produce enough electricity in a large atomic plant to serve a modern city of twenty million people for a full year. Likewise, the micro particles released with the fumes of an agnihotra yagya interact with all the five elements of nature, producing and bringing back beneficial products powerfully and abundantly.

Chapter 18

The Fruits of Yagya

Yagyashishtashina santo muchyantey sarvakilvishay,
Bhunjatey te twagham papa ye pachyantya aatmakaaranaat.

Shri Krishna: *A person who shares the proceeds of yagya with other participants, delivers himself from sins, but one who prepares food only for himself or partakes of food himself without serving others is committing sins.*

In this verse is given the entire secret of human prosperity and lasting happiness. A person who performs a yagya but tries to accumulate the material proceeds of the yagya commits a sin. Sharing the proceeds liberally and rightfully, on the contrary, delivers him from sins. Delivered from sins, his desires are fulfilled one by one and he eventually attains lasting happiness.

Yajurveda, the primeval human scripture, is replete with praises of yagya in its verses. The Creator has set in his vast universe the inviolable law of cause and effect. Whatever you give to the universe comes back to you in both qualitative and quantitative terms. If you help the needy in their times of crisis, help will come back to you when you face similar situations. If you serve your parents well, you too will be looked after well by your children. If you treat your peers courteously, you will get courtesy back from them. If you try to dodge and deceive others, people will treat you with scepticism and you will become the target of crooked designs of some of them. If you mollify the living beings—the plants, trees and animals—their Creator will satisfy your needs. If you invest money and efforts in a business scheme for extending any kinds of benefits to others, you will get back benefits as profits. If you purify the air through agnihotra yagya, you purify the minds, bodies and intellects of many other humans and also lesser beings using that vital natural element. Purifying the minds, bodies and intellects of other human beings will result in refinement of their karmas and will enhance peace and harmony in the human society. It will make the environment more conducive to progress and prosperity. You too will be rewarded for this noble karma with peace and prosperity. The reward will be bestowed by the Creator whose divine will runs through the universe, with undercurrents of perfect justice.

In the modern corporate business environment where we find various types of corporate cultures, the similar thing holds good for relationship of business houses with their customers. In some business houses, employees are liberally rewarded with promotions, increments and bonuses in times of boom as well as in regular times, whereas some business houses are stingy in sharing profits with employees. The more you give and the more you share, the more you get back. The fruits of yagya come back to the performer qualitatively and quantitatively in unmistakable terms.

We need to realize the fundamental truth that wealth is not meant to be accumulated or hoarded. It is required to be spent in useful and productive activities. While madly pursuing wealth in the present times, we forget that we do not know what we are going to do with it. To quote the ecological economist, Tim Jackson, 'We spend money we don't have on things we don't need to create impressions that won't last on people we don't care about.' Wealth is not an entity with a positive attribute. It is neither positive nor negative. It is neutral. How we earn it and how we employ it are of greater consequence. Truly, it is how we use wealth which makes it useful or harmful.

All awards and rewards, bounties, gains—petty or windfall—medals, prizes and profits that we get in life are the fruits of yagya. Hence to get any or more of these, you need to serve others, deliver benefits to others and nourish the nature's ecosystem.

Drawing upon the message of this verse, modern man must realize the core spiritual truth that all his material rewards come from the realm of the Almighty through the working of the process of yagya in which rewards flow back inexorably to the performer and the participant in the collective human activity beneficial to all. In this activity, the more one gives to others for their benefits, the more one becomes entitled to get from the universe. Hence, today's man should become service-oriented and selfless in his approach to get material benefits for himself. In other words, following the principle of caring and sharing is the sign of a good life. That is what we all should endeavour to do to uplift our lives.

Whatever applies to a human individual, applies, through analogy, to a family, a social service club, a business house or a government. The more sincerely and extensively these institutions work for the benefits of the persons served by them, the more rich and resourceful they grow in keeping with the spiritual principles underlying yagya. We are witness to corrupt regimes getting weak and uprooted, while nations who care for their citizens through the well-oiled machinery of taxation and social benefits delivery growing rich and powerful. The message of the fruits of yagya truly forms the philosophical foundation of human prosperity.

Chapter 19

The Importance of Varnadharma

Shreyaan swadharmo vigunah pardharmaat swanushthitaat,
Swadharmey nidhanam shreya pardharmo bhayavaha.

Shri Krishna: *You should try to perform assiduously your own varnadharma, i.e. the vocational duty corresponding to your varna.* It is far better to perform your own varnadharma, even if it appears to be improper to do so at certain times, than other's varnadharma even though the latter may appear to be the right thing to do at that time. It is better to fearlessly die performing one's own varnadharma than to perform other's varnadharma, which generates fear.*

The importance of varnadharma has been delineated in the Vedas, the primeval scriptures. Every human being ushered into this world has guna, karma and swabhav (nature and attributes) that can categorize him as a brahmin, kshatriya, vaishya or shudra. Therefore, he belongs to one of these four varnas and each varna is characterized by its own set of avocations that sustain the human society through time continuum.

---

*Occupational caste

The almighty Creator has made all men equal but not similar. Their innate physical and mental qualities are different. A mix of these qualities makes a person composed, patient, inquisitive and intelligent. Such a person belongs to the brahman varna. Another has attributes that make him bold, strong and just. Such a person is categorized as a kshatriya. A third one is honest, calculative, courteous and industrious. He is a vaishya by varna. The fourth category of shudra is characterized by the qualities of humility, subservience and faithfulness.

What happens when one forsakes his varna-linked duties? He undermines peace and harmony of the society because he is not doing justice to his God-ordained role in the human society. This God-ordained role is nothing but varnadharma. In other words, one should perform a vocational role in line with his natural qualities and aptitude, which is his God-ordained duty. That will enable him to give his best to the society and, accordingly, will be best conducive to welfare and growth of all members of the society. Taking up a role not in line with one's varnadharma will make him a square peg in a round hole. As a misfit in that role, his engagement will create tension and stress in the society. Shri Krishna, in this verse, has pointedly mentioned this.

Modern management only upholds and corroborates the above statements. It talks of skills, like verbal, mathematical, spatial and reasoning—terms most commonly met with in aptitude tests prescribed for Management schools. Modern human resource development (HRD) practitioners of the corporate world also talk of attributes like 'emotional quotient'. We find, in today's world, professionals called career counsellors. They identify the appropriate career of an individual having regard to these inherent abilities and aptitudes, which they measure through specialized tests. Many of the attributes so measured are innate in an individual, though they can be polished and improved to limited extents. Varnadharma is the set of avocations tailor-made for a person with a given aptitude and basic skill profile. Hence, varnadharma is important.

The concept of varnadharma is closely linked with natural aptitudes of individuals, who need to identify early in life their lines of interest and aptitude and then take up education, training and occupations accordingly. This way, they will get maximum benefits, while extending maximum benefits to the society.

Sachin Tendulkar dropped out of high school to concentrate on cricket. He went on to become a legendary cricket player. Amitabh Bachchan was a corporate salesperson in Kolkata. He quit his job to pursue a career in acting, the field where his interest actually lay. He went on to become a Bollywood superstar. There are numerous examples of persons who chose to work in their fields of interest, ignoring all extraneous factors and remarkably shone in those fields, setting benchmarks of excellence for generations to come.

It is, therefore, important to follow varnadharma which is in accordance with one's innate characteristics and the designs set forth by nature. It optimizes one's contribution and utility to the society and the world at large. Today, the entire world is grappling with the problem of economic recession and the resultant incidence of unemployment. Much of it is attributable to automation and information technology advancement. We hear of unmanned cars and trucks already constructed and tested by manufacturing companies. We are already witness to robots working in place of humans at the shop floors of factories. Areas where humans have natural interest and aptitude are the areas where they need to be trained. Skill sets should be imparted in accordance with one's aptitudes. That will produce persons eager to work for their own satisfaction, rather than merely for a living. Jobs will become enjoyable rather than remaining stereotyped and dull. People will become more productive and innovative. That will provide a fillip to research and development. That will create more jobs and improve the economic climate. This, in brief, is the practical message that this verse brings out.

Chapter 20

The Past Connection

Bahuni me yvyatitaani janmaani tag cha Arjun,
Tanyaham ved sarvaani natwam vettha parantap.

Shri Krishna: *O Arjun, you and me have lived many different lives in the past. I know the account of each one of them but you don't.*

There is a past connection to every present event. The birth of each one of us is also an event with a past historical link. Nothing in this universe that pertains to a sentient being happens in a purely random manner. There is always a divine design to it. This, quite logically, follows from the law of cause and effect or the universal law of retribution. Our karmas are the cause-seeds and these seeds will germinate into karma-trees, and eventually bear fruit. Events in life that impact us qualitatively are these fruits.

If you are enjoying abundant wealth, be sure that you have been honest and hardworking in your past life. If you are suffering from penury, unmistakably you have indulged in economic corruption in your previous life. If you are suffering from ill health, you must have violated the laws of natural living in the immediate past. If you are occupying a position of high status and power, you must have lived a humble life and served others with dedication in the past.

As mentioned in the above examples, there is a definite past connection to every event in the present life of a person in qualitative as well as quantitative terms. But ordinary human beings have short memories. The previous life affairs are erased from their memories. Exception to this are yogis and liberated souls who have attained salvation and are reborn for some sublime objectives. Shri Krishna was one such soul. Through his yogic powers, he was able to see the events in the previous lives of Arjun as well as his own. By visualizing the events and activities in the past lives of both, he was able to understand why Arjun was pitched in the battle of Mahabharat against his cousins and his respected teacher.

Ordinary human beings are not able to see their previous life events because their limited knowledge would make them question the designs of destiny and make their present moments painful. They would question the propriety of these designs and find themselves unable to reconcile with the sequence of their life events because of their innately imperfect knowledge and understanding. The yogis possess clear and perfect understanding of things and they would understand the divine design behind the chain of events which possesses the undercurrents of seamless justice.

This verse of the Bhagwadgita brings out the above message and explains to humans why they do not remember their past life events or actions. It makes them live in the present which is required for their actual progress.

Even in the modern society, we have witnessed a special breed of psychologists and psychotherapists who perform 'past life regression analysis'. They are skilled in the technique of taking a person, through the hypnotic mechanism, into his past life, impressions of which lie deeply buried in his subconscious mind. In many cases, they are able to elucidate a well-meaning connection between past life actions and present life events. The important point in this regard is that our past actions create many of the present circumstances, situations and events—good or bad, favourable or unfavourable. But this does not mean that we are prisoners of our past. We can alter the currents of destiny through well-guided and well-directed efforts. The concept of past connection should get firmly embedded in our minds, so that we may appreciate the importance of karma and its short- or long-term repercussions. Once we comprehend the great importance of karma in human life, we will be on the right track. We shall, no doubt, advance forward successfully in the arduous but exciting journey called life.

Modern man should imbibe the message of living in the present and for the day from this verse. Let bygones be bygones. The past is an 'expired cheque'. The future is a 'postdated cheque'. The present is a gift. Live in the present and for the day, forgetting about the past and without worrying about the future. The very fact that we do not remember events of our past lives indicates that the Creator does not intend his human subjects to carry memories of the past life events. Such memories will interfere with their free and unattached working in the present life. They will be a hurdle in their spiritual growth. That is why we humans just need to forget about our past and concentrate on the present. Doing so embodies the principles of good living.

Chapter 21

Reincarnation for Divine Purpose

Yada yada hi dharmasya glanirbhawati bharat,
Abhutthanam dharmasya tadatmanam srijamyaham,
Paritranaya sadhunaam vinashaya cha dushkritaam.
Dharmasanstha punatthaya sambhawami yugey yugey.

Shri Krishna: *O Bharat, whenever dharma is at a low ebb in the world, I am reborn as a human being in every aeon to resurrect dharma, to support noble persons, to decimate the evil persons and to re-establish institutions of dharma.*

Liberated souls are free of any blemish. They possess complete and correct understanding of all things. They have no natural inclination towards any type of wrong and sinful conduct. They are in complete tuning with the almighty power, God. They have developed extraordinary powers, unimaginable for ordinary human beings. They can gaze through the past and can tap the infinite spiritual power of the almighty Creator at will. Fully accomplished in yoga of the body, mind and intellect, they are free to roam around the vast universe in their non-corporeal state. The Creator does not need to give them corporeal existence except for special purposes. These special purposes are errands to correct the distortions in the human society caused by the unrighteous conduct of ordinary, unenlightened human beings. As the liberated souls are enlightened and accomplished, they appear to have supernatural powers. Shri Krishna was one such soul.

Towards the end of the previous era of Dwapar, depravation in the human society had reached strikingly high levels. True knowledge belonging to the realm of the Vedas was being ignored, diluted or distorted and precepts to hold the society in peace and harmony were not in place. In the wake of this obscurantism, corruption in peoples' thoughts, behaviour and actions had led to widespread malaise. Moral degradation manifesting in greed and treachery had eroded honesty and truthfulness in human conduct. Institutions did not uphold the principles of dharma and did not, accordingly, deliver justice to persons served by them. It was exactly in these circumstances that high, emancipated souls like Shri Krishna took human birth to bring back order, harmony and peace in the human society.

Since liberated souls, like Shri Krishna, are in full sync with God, the supreme spiritual entity, they can never do any act in violation of the eternal laws set by Him and whatever they do can be considered as the action of God. It is exactly in this context that Shri Krishna has stated that he incarnates in special circumstances and the mission behind this incarnation is divine, dedicated to resurrection of peace, order and righteousness.

Every soul has a past connection, and actions and activities of the past determine events in the future. Shri Krishna, in his past life, had attained salvation. His rebirth as a human being was designed and decreed by the Almighty for a very special purpose indeed. This special purpose was re-establishment of dharma in the human society. Resurrection of dharma often needs a 'surgical operation' when evil forces of the society become powerful. Shri Krishna guided Arjun and his Pandava kinsmen to victory in the epic battle.

The verse carries two sublime messages for contemporary humans.

The first is that true religion is the religion of humanity. Today's world presents an ironical picture of sects and cults by the thousands in the name of religion, but humanism at a premium. Great men and women who adorn the earth from time to time set examples of actions worthy of emulation by others. The names Abraham Lincoln, Mahatma Gandhi and Nelson Mandela are synonymous with humanism. Their actions for promotion of dharma continue to be object lessons for all. Their lives were a relentless struggle against injustice and evil. We should also endeavour to uphold righteousness and humanism, wherever we may live and irrespective of our caste, creed, race or nationality. We should selflessly and fearlessly support noble persons, persons who are morally upright and humanistic. And we need to oppose corrupt and morally depraved persons. That way, we shall continuously aid in the maintenance of order and harmony in the global society.

We should propagate the religion of humanity.

The other uplifting message that emerges from this verse is that the teachings of high souls, like Shri Krishna, are universal and time-tested. We should apply them liberally in every situation and at every time, as required. Shri Krishna's life was a saga of struggle against the enemies of dharma. He exemplified the ideals of love, equality and justice in his interaction with others. In the contemporary society, we observe that a larger proportion of people is self-centered. Institutions—political, economic, academic or legal—are growing more complex but do not show a growing focus on promoting humanism. Selfless and altruistic persons are relatively few. In such times, Shri Krishna's message is more than relevant. We need to work relentlessly against evil forces and try to establish justice by peaceful means as far as possible. If peaceful means do not work, we should be prepared to wage an all-out war against the enemies of dharma in order to bring about durable peace and order in the world.

Chapter 22

Birth and Life of a Yogi

Janma karm cha mey diwyamewam yo vetti tattwata,
Tyaktwa deham punarjanma naiti maameti so Arjun,
Na maamkarmani limpanti na mey karmphaley spriha.

Shri Krishna: My birth, life and actions are of a special, divine character because my actions do not cast any impressions on me nor do I get entrenched in their effects. One who understands these facts does not get reborn after casting off his physical body but attains tuning with God, the supreme spiritual entity.

A yogi is one who, by following the scientific principles governing matter and spirit, optimizes the use of his physical, mental and intellectual faculties. He acquires strength, power, stamina and endurance much beyond the ordinary. He fully understands the tenets of dharma and abides by them quite naturally and instinctively. His proclivity for unrighteous action has been reduced to zero. He is a fully refined and polished personality. His actions are selfless and outlook, altruistic.

A person with the above attributes is born with no baggage of positive or negative karmas of the past life with retributive effects nor does such a person have any remnant material desires to fulfil. Even during the term of the special life appearance that he has taken, he remains completely free from any material desires. All his karmas are performed to fulfil sublime objectives.

Ordinary human beings do not possess a practical understanding of the above-mentioned facts of human existence and continue to remain in the rigmarole of desires and aspirations of the mundane world and of retributive effects of positive and negative karmas fuelled by desires. Accordingly, an ordinary person does not attain human perfection and tuning with his spiritual master and creator, God. He is reborn.

In today's life, we humans perform many qualitatively good or bad actions for specific purposes. Some of our actions, like those involving infidelity, corruption or treachery, inflict harm on others and are performed for bringing benefits to us in a devious manner. Some of the actions, like charity work, are qualitatively good and are deliberately done for reaping rich material rewards in terms of name or recognition. In either case, there is an element of selfishness attached to our action, and such actions unfailingly cast impressions on us which get us caught in their retributive effects. Such actions are not liberating.

A person who has experienced, through his sublime actions, that karmas which do not cast lasting impressions on human subconscious mind are devoid of attachment and will not engender mundane fruits, has understood the fundamental truth of life. He comes in the bracket of yogis. He is able to successfully sever his connection with the world of mortal beings.

The life of a yogi is an object lesson in optimal utilization of human faculties and available resources for the ordinary humans. It provides practical guidance to humans in leading productive and fulfilling lives. The life of a yogi is a trail of events which illustrate the working of the human soul in unison with its Master, the infinite superior soul of the universe.

We only have to go through the biographical accounts of remarkable persons of history to appreciate the above statement. Their lives are tales of struggle, strife, perseverance, defiance of injustice and sacrifice. Many of these great persons have faced more trials and tribulations in life than the ordinary persons. But the ways in which they have overcome obstacles and challenges become eloquent expressions of the sublime actions that lead to human liberation. The lives of Nichiren Daishonin, Jesus Christ, Galileo Galilei and Nelson Mandela are standing testimonies to the power of faith or scientific truth or justice. These famous men faced incarceration and suffering at the hands of the society, but they clung on to the values they were professing and the causes they were espousing. Each life account teaches us to live with devotion to the immanent, eternal truths that govern life.

Even in the present times, persons who demonstrate extraordinary patience, stamina, steadfastness and truthfulness at once command reverence because these are the attributes of a yogi. Getting over the mental frailties that characterize ordinary humans makes a person a yogi. Yes, the yogi is an extraordinary human being.

The sequence of events in the life history of a yogi reinforces the faith of ordinary human mortals in God and makes them more spiritually inclined. It makes them more dharma-oriented and helps to enhance happiness and peace in the global human society. That is why Shri Krishna and his actions, his philosophy and his life principles are still alive today, 5,100 years after his death at the end of the Dwapar era. They continue to serve as a beacon of divine light to the present-age humans, struggling and striving for a better life, as always.

Chapter 23

Right Knowledge, Right Action

Karmanyakarm ya pashyed karmani cha karm yah,
Sa buddhimaan manushyeshu sa yuktah kritsnakarma krit.

Shri Krishna: *A person who possesses the understanding of right knowledge and right action and also understands the eternal relationship between specific strands of knowledge and actions based on them is a yogi, and such a person performs all actions right.*

Here Shri Krishna emphasizes on the importance of right knowledge and human action in accordance with such knowledge. Right knowledge exists eternally as true core knowledge with its explanations and corollaries. Action based only on such knowledge is beneficial. Action not in accordance with such knowledge generates disharmony, tension and conflict and leaves deleterious consequences.

What is right knowledge?

It is that knowledge which is sourced to the almighty Creator, devoid of dilution or distortion. Such knowledge exists in the Vedas, the eternal, primeval scriptures. The Vedas are the words of God revealed to the earliest humans for posterity.

Human action in line with such knowledge is right action. Right knowledge is scientific and logical. Right action is objective and its result predictable. Right knowledge is factual and consistent with realities of the universe. Right action is that which, if followed, promotes peace and progress.

In the present world too, we observe multiple ideologies and schools of thought. There exists a huge number of religions, identified by prime religions and their variants, with a wide number of cults and sects. Their ideologies have similarities as well as sharp differences. Sourced to the core knowledge enshrined in the Vedas with explanations performed objectively, these ideologies remain like strands of right knowledge. Following them, humans will always live in total peace and harmony. Right knowledge truly emancipates man and frees him from pain and privation.

At the more earthly level, right knowledge connotes complete knowledge based on rational understanding. It precludes knowledge which is based on superstition, blind faith, rumours or heresay. It excludes knowledge not based on scientific analysis of things. Right knowledge acts as a catalyst for human success. Half knowledge or knowledge not based on intelligent logic lands humans in marshy soils and not only impedes progress, but is also regressive.

In today's world, we humans are not exploiting our physical and mental faculties by more than 5 per cent. Raising this use of faculties is possible through yoga. The key to material and spiritual progress is the combination of right knowledge and right action. Right knowledge is the knowledge sourced to the Vedas, which are divinely revealed, and right action is action consonant with the Vedas. Hence, if we practice right knowledge, we shall elevate ourselves. We shall become yogis.

The yogi acquires physical and mental strength far more

than that exhibited by ordinary human beings. He possesses an intellectual faculty which is far superior to that of the ordinary person. He can perform extraordinary physical and mental feats. The word 'superman' does not come from the realm of fantasy. The yogi is a superman.

In today's world, the concept of right knowledge is debatable and is bound to attract controversy. Every ideological school thinks its ideology to be the gospel of truth and other ideologies to be untruth or collection of half-truths. Under such circumstances, it is wise to leave rational judgement as the criterion to test the veracity of any ideological strand. Every human being is endowed with the power to make a dispassionate analysis of any issue or subject. Hence, developing a more rational perspective is the way to get the best out of life. With this approach, modern humans can tap the power of eternal knowledge which is enshrined in the Vedas, while also continuously deciphering the ubiquitous signs and symbols in nature which convey right knowledge.

Understanding of right knowledge is not enough in practical life. Humans know that it pays to abide by truth. Everyone knows that practice makes a man perfect. It is widely believed that a bad temper is damaging for relationships. And yes, perseverance brings rewards inevitably. But getting the human act together to live truthfully, behave politely and work hard is challenging. It needs the knowledge of application, of regulation of the mind. That is where the knowledge of right action comes useful. Modern life has become complex and challenging. People require the knowledge of mind training today, perhaps more than they ever did. This verse of the Bhagwadgita tells us the importance of knowledge of both theory and application.

The understanding of something called right knowledge will make ordinary humans dispersed across the globe more eager to search for truth and facts, irrespective of their faiths. They will become more rational and scientific in their approach. This will be conducive to unity and harmony among the global community members.

Chapter 24

Mental Equanimity: The Key to Liberation

Yadrichhalabh santushto dwandwatito vimatsara,
Sama siddhawasiddhow cha kritwapi na nibhadhyatey.

Shri Krishna: *A person who remains satisfied with whatever he gets from the realm of the Creator, who has risen above the mundane dualities of life and views success and failure alike is an enlightened person and through his actions, he does not get entrapped in the vortex of divine retribution of karmas.*

Unattached karma, i.e. karma without obsession for material reward or result, is the key to human salvation. This divine message is put forward by this verse. A person who possesses unflinching faith in the justice of the Almighty will always welcome happy or sad events in his life as the retributive effects of his past actions, coming from the Creator whose justice is impeccable. He is aligned to the core truth of the operation of this vast universe. Hence, he views all dualities of life, like success-failure, pleasure-pain, loss-gain, infamy-fame, etc. with a balanced perspective. He does not jump in happiness at winning a jackpot nor sink into despair at the loss of his job. Equanimity of the mind is the hallmark of his personality.

How does man attain the above mental state? The Vedas say that man should lead a perseverant life, with actions based on true knowledge. If you endeavour to live even one day or half a day or even two hours of your life with this approach, you will appreciate the divine truth pronounced by the Vedas. You will derive a different kind of happiness out of your unattached work. This happiness is sublime and comes to the hard-working student, to the toiling peasant, to the patriotic soldier and to the statesman–politician working with an altruistic, missionary spirit. They are working selflessly and that makes their actions unattached.

Mental equanimity in a person means he never feels high or low, but always remains calm and composed. It means he has risen above the states of gloominess and frustration over unfavourable events and it also means he has risen above the feelings of excitement and exultation over favourable happenings. What he experiences at all times is a feeling of satisfaction and contentment. This feeling is elevating and divine. In such a state of the mind, he is free from both fear and worry. Such state is the springboard to human liberation.

Bridling the errant mind is always a challenging ordeal. But it is possible by sustained practice. A person who exercises control over the excitable mind becomes a performer and a winner all the way. These days, psychologists and sociologists use a term called emotional quotient in this regard. A person with high emotional quotient is said to be more balanced and rational in his actions. Yes, he has better control over his mind. Mind is, after all, the gateway to heavens and also the doorway to hell.

We pick up a great teaching from this verse—that of increasing our emotional quotient, that of living by reason rather than by emotion. It tells us not to jump in jubilation at the turnout of happy events or to become downcast at the sad events of life. If we follow this message in word and deed, we shall refine our personalities and elevate the quality of our karmas. What do we witness in today's global society? People celebrate success by throwing gala parties and hosting ostentatious shows. At failures, people become quiet, gloomy and go into seclusion. Either action is irrational and not in sync with the true nature of man and his Creator. People live by emotion more than by reason.

The game of cricket is a rage in the Indian subcontinent. One remembers how in Pakistan, the losing national cricket team members were booed and stones and brickbats were thrown at their houses. On the contrary, members of the national team emerging winners in the world cup were felicitated by bursting crackers and huge adulatory shows on the roads and streets of cities.

Not getting euphoric in success and not getting despondent in failure is the sign of an emotionally matured person. Success and failure are really two faces of the same coin. Both come from the realm of the Creator. Therefore, we should be accepting them gracefully, without losing our mental composure.

For an individual, failure is an event to introspect and by doing so, he begins to get over his weaknesses that caused the failure. Success is, for a balanced individual, an event to thank the Creator and other people for support, motivation and co-operation which led to his success. This way, success will never go to his head. And for the person who failed, this approach will truly make him learn from failure to emerge a winner the next time.

The Essence of Bhagwadgita 83

Chapter 25

The Yagya Performer

Dravya yagyasta poyagyaa yogayagyasta tha aparey,
Swadhyaya yagyaan yagyaasch yataya sanshita vrataa.

Shri Krishna: *Many such persons called Yatis perform intensive yagyas like agnihotra yagya, charity, virtuous actions and participatory activities for collective benefits, including severe penance for others' welfare. Many others undertake religious discourse and dissemination of divine knowledge.*

Yagya is a soul-elevating activity. It bestows on the performer peace and prosperity. Persons who have mental equipoise are regularly engaged in yagyas of various types that bring material and spiritual benefits to living beings. The agnihotra yagya involves oblation to fire. Such oblations consist of offerings of natural substances that purify the environment. Substances like pure ghee derived from cow's milk, aromatic herbs and camphor when offered to the fire, are split into subtle micro particles that ascend with the fumes and purify the physical environment. In specific terms, they purify the five basic elements of nature—earth, water, fire, air and ether. These five elements are the constituents of the body, mind and intellect of every living being.

Purification of the five basic elements, in turn, purifies the minds, bodies and intellects of living beings, which improves their health and refines their karmas. The refinement of karmas brings them peace, progress and prosperity. The fact of refinement of karmas is based on the understanding that human actions are motivated by their minds and guided by their intellects. If mind and intellect work well, human actions will be in line with the eternal laws of the universe. They will be conducive to peace and stability. They will enhance human happiness.

There are many other types of yagya. Charitable activities—giving alms to the poor, undertaking philanthropic projects, supporting causes for helping the physically and mentally challenged persons are also yagyas. All virtuous human actions are yagyas. All such actions assuage the sufferings of people and promote their welfare in some way or the other.

Yagya leaves a trail of beneficial effects. This great truth can be understood by citing a few facts. The agnihotra yagya, which purifies the air, works according to scientific principles. The fumes from the yagya fire that rise into the atmosphere are so powerful that every cubic metre of fumes purifies a million cubic metres of air. Modern scientists are still far away from a comprehension of this phenomenon. This yagya is the ultimate depolluting measure. In today's times, when the physical environment has become so degraded, agnihotra yagya is the answer to global environmental pollution. We can surely prevent the impending environmental disaster looming large over us through this measure expounded in the Yajurveda.

At the individual or collective level, yagya, as a participative activity, brings back benefits galore to the performer. Running a business venture, investing time and efforts to help orphans or physically handicapped children, undertaking scientific research and development work, spreading the message of divine scriptures, serving the government of the country, raising a family, etc. are all further examples in yagya, where you offer something and get benefits in return from the universe. The more you offer, the more you get back.

Bill Gates, the founder of Microsoft Corporation, remarked that he had failed in a few subjects in his high school. His classmate, on the other hand, passed in all courses. Gates stated that, later, while his classmate was an employee at Microsoft, he was the owner of the corporation. The reason—Bill Gates performed a much bigger yagya by developing original softwares and catering to the global community.

The more you offer, the more you get back. The universe returns to you precisely what you give it. The long hours that are spent in your professional work, the time devoted to passionate social service, the money given in charity, the days and months of struggle against social evils and human injustice and the activities performed for promotion of peace and harmony are all oblations in yagya that will bring forth benefits to you in precise measures.

Yagya benefits all the participants and uplifts them. With this approach and the attitude of a yagya performer, we should carry out our mundane actions. Every activity that we perform should be intended for promoting the welfare of other living beings. In that case, we shall hardly waver from the right course—we shall not commit sins, wittingly or unwittingly. Our actions shall always be conducive to peace and universal welfare.

Chapter 26

Knowledge and Evolution

Sarva karmakhilam parth gyaney parisamapyatey,
Tadwidwi pranipaatein pariprashnein sewaya.

Shri Krishna: *All types of actions end in enlightenment or true knowledge attainment. To acquire such knowledge and understanding, pay obeisance to erudite scholars. Please them through service and seek from them answers to your questions. Thus you will acquire pure knowledge.*

Shri Krishna conveys through this verse the message that the ultimate objective of human life is to attain enlightenment or true knowledge. Whatever qualitative actions that a human being performs at the gross mundane level or at the mental level are retributory and these retributory effects make the action performing person more experienced. Greater experience gives him a clearer perspective on things. This is like getting enlightened to truth in that area. Once he is enlightened in a certain sphere, he attains incremental spiritual elevation.

The human being has incomplete knowledge, understanding and intellectual capability. This limitation is so grave that millions of humans over hundreds and thousands of years can remain ignorant of divine truths and realities of life. They can continue to wallow in illusion. That is precisely the reason why their Creator has handed down to them true knowledge through the scriptures called the Vedas. But human beings, for what they are, often ignore or misread or misinterpret the scriptural messages and suffer the baneful consequences thereof.

Every action ends in understanding or knowledge gain. A man eats food and when he feels his hunger has been appeased, he stops eating. A person who has booked air travel tickets enters an aircraft and after the flight lands, he comes out of the aircraft with the understanding that his destination has arrived. These are very simple examples of mundane actions. Qualitative actions, which benefit or harm other beings, bring retributive effects on the human performer after some time, depending upon the type of action. Virtuous karmas bring material rewards and refinement of spiritual knowledge. Sinful deeds bring sorrow but these sorrows and miseries also refine human understanding of spiritual truths. Thus, divine retribution of karmas, in all cases, elevates humans spiritually. Learned persons are the source of divine knowledge for ordinary and less than ordinary humans who cannot read or understand scriptures.

This verse tells us the importance of teacher or preceptor in life. Learned scholars help us to understand strands of knowledge which we are unable to absorb directly from books. They explain to us the meaning and import of scriptural hymns, many of which appear to be esoteric. They guide us towards comprehension of the divine principles of evolution and performance of karmas in accordance with those principles. They help us to practise those principles and precepts. Practice leads to experiential knowledge which refines us spiritually.

In today's society, the respect for teacher or 'guru' seems to be waning. It is not difficult to see that many people, at every age and stage of life, are driven by arrogance and egotism and not by an honest, humble desire to learn from elders and more experienced folks. This is rather unfortunate. Today, a great section of youngsters thinks that its elders are fools, mired in orthodoxy. These youngsters refuse to imbibe the valuable lessons of life from the older generation, lessons which can catalyze their evolution. This verse brings a great life-elevating message for them. Since we all are of limited knowledge and understanding, we learn from the erudite folks, from the more experienced and knowledgeable ones. To acquire knowledge thus, we need to cultivate humility because egotism is the biggest hindrance in learning. Elders are more experienced folks and life-elevating knowledge is gained experientially. That is why we must respect the elderly, because we will always have a thing or two to learn from them.

Notwithstanding the above, we need to respect the knowledgeable and the experienced folks in general because knowledge and experience do not necessarily belong to those who have lived more years. Age is no bar to learning, and a younger person can have more knowledge and experience in certain domains than the older ones. We, in general, should cultivate a culture of respect for the knowledgeable persons. They should not be treated as just errand boys, even if they are employed as such.

Knowledge is the foundation of human evolution and knowledge is not under the ownership of any person or set of persons. All knowledge is sourced to God and we humans are only deciphering, interpreting and implementing it from time to time.

Indeed, Shri Krishna has encapsulated the entire philosophy of human evolution in this verse. It illumines the path of learning and human development.

Chapter 27

Renunciation and Righteous Action

Sanyasa karmayogashcha nishreyaskarawubhau,
Tasyostu karma sanyasaat karmayogo vishishyatey.

Shri Krishna: *Renunciation and righteous karma both give sublime benefits, but of the two, righteous karmas bring greater benefits.*

Renunciation is the relinquishment of earthly desire. It cuts at the roots of human attachment with mundane affairs. It brings the human soul closer to the supreme Creator since it provides a more realistic perspective on life and its objective. A person who performs his worldly actions with a mental frame of detachment enjoys his actions without expectation of material rewards. He does expect spiritual rewards, which means he desires benefits to accrue to other persons and beings. His perspective is selfless.

Righteous karmas are karmas in line with dharma. Such actions by a person inexorably bring him positive retributive effects. He gets material bounties as rewards for his actions. These benefits include accrual of money, fame and general prosperity but he remains exposed to the temptations of the material world which fuel the fire of greed. Human mind, with its inherent frailties, tends to give in and the person often becomes a slave to banal elements of passion and desire. In such a case, his karmas could be apparently right but do not remain fully righteous. He sometimes slips into the vortex of desire which slows down his evolution.

Renunciation provides a different route to liberation. It gives a fast track to salvation of the human being. Doing karmas for sublime benefits brings gains in greater measure than performance of karmas for gross material gains.

Renunciation brings a person closer to the core realities of existence. In accordance with these realities, a human being should always keep in his mind that he is essentially a speck of spiritual element seeking knowledge, fulfilment and deliverance from sorrow. His Creator is a superior spirit, infinite in extent and expanse. Attachment with material objects provides fodder to the monster of material desire. That only works to further entangle a person in the labyrinth of mundane karmas and their inexorable effects. His actual liberation is put off in time. Thus, in terms of core fundamentals of existence, one should aspire and strive for higher goals of life which will bring greater benefits, in both quantitative and qualitative terms.

Renunciation opens up to the human soul the pathway to perfection. It reveals to a person his true sense of being and his real objective in life. It makes him aware of the existential realities of eternal life and strengthens his connection with the Almighty. It is the first step in the process of human emancipation. But renunciation cannot be at the cost of our solemn duty as responsible citizens. We cannot abdicate our duties and be called righteous.

Right karmas are objective and rational actions. They undoubtedly bring results to the performer but they may or may not be fully in line with dharma. In modern life, we are witness to the growing strength, power and clout of various types of mafia groups—in business, politics and elsewhere. We observe international terrorist outfits growing and creating havoc. We are also privy to trade unions, interest groups, pressure groups, etc. at work to further the interests of small community sections served by them, often to the detriment of the larger human institutions. The actions of such groups may be right and productive but not necessarily righteous. They may not be productive and beneficial in the longer run.

As explained above, this verse teaches the contemporary human being to be righteous, above all. Renunciation is meaningful when we have reached the right stage of our life after performing our mundane duties or when we have reached a stage of evolution after relinquishment of desire. Righteousness or dharma has a very universal definition. It transcends the differences of race, geographical location, language, religion or culture. The defining principles of dharma propounded in the *Manusmriti* in the form of a ten-point code state that a human being must practise the following:

- Forgiveness
- Patience
- Truthfulness
- Mind control
- Honesty
- Cleanliness of body and mind
- Acquiring true knowledge
- Intellectual application
- Control of the senses
- Abjuring anger

Following the above universal code of religion is the pathway to success, happiness and salvation. Hence, when we fail in our endeavours, the cause of failure is invariably our non-observance of one or more code points mentioned above. We can introspect and see which code point of dharma was not observed by us. If we follow the above code comprehensively, we can never ever fail. It is easy to see that the above ten-point code is not sectarian or communal in character. It is spiritual and universalistic and hence is applicable to the entire humanity. It is the code of action for human upliftment, success, happiness and glory. It can act as the peace-promoting potion in today's world that is stricken by grave tension and disharmony in its many pockets.

Chapter 28

The Yoga of Knowledge

Yogayukto munirbramha na chirenadhigachhati,
Sarwabhutaatma bhutaatma kurwannapi na lipyatey.

Shri Krishna: *Those accomplished in gyan yoga* attain union with God faster because they develop a realistic perspective of seeing the omnipresent, universal spirit in all beings and hence they do not fall in the vortex of retributive effects of their karmas.*

When a person becomes aware of the metaphysical reality that the Creator and Regulator of the universe exists eternally as an infinite spiritual power pervading all and everything, including the physical bodies and souls of all living beings, he begins to view his entire life in that perspective. He remains continually alive to the ultimate reality that his physical body is only a temporary sheath provided to him to perform his karmas and attain enlightenment in incremental steps. These are the steps in his evolution that will ultimately take him to the stage of salvation.

---

*Yoga of knowledge

Let us, for the sake of examples, consider the cases of a professional engineer, doctor, politician, teacher and trader businessman. Each one is performing his own professional activity in the society for earning money. But if each one has developed gyan yoga, he will perform his work with the prime objective of extending maximum benefits to the customers served by him. Earning money will be a secondary objective. He will have the understanding and realization that wealth will inevitably flow to him through his actions. Thus, the engineer will try to construct that overbridge without time and cost overrun and maintain utmost standards of quality. The doctor will focus on healing his patient thoroughly and quickly; he will be compassionate and not commercial in his approach. A politician of that category will work for the welfare of his voters and not for consolidation of his vote banks. He will indulge in politics of popular welfare and not in politics of vote. The teacher will focus on the task of achieving the best grades for his students, and not undertake private tuitions. A businessman of this category, trading in commodities, will seek to serve his customers with best quality goods and timely deliveries, rather than maximizing profits for his own self.

In all the above cases, a person striving for benefits of others and sharing the gains reasonably gets maximum benefits through the divine law of cause and effect operated by the Creator. He behaves so because he is focused on true knowledge and bases his actions on such knowledge. The rewards of such actions demonstrate the power of true knowledge. Such rewards are balanced, abundant and fulfilling.

Let us cast a look at the modern scientific community and scientific practice. The community of scientists largely believes that facts are those that are evident or are testable by experiments. They discount and disbelieve whatever is not perceived through the human senses helped by scientific devices. Many drugs of allopathic practice, like Aspirin and Enteroquinol, which were freely prescribed fifty years ago, are now banned by the medical community because of serious side effects. The community still refuses to believe that quelling the symptoms of diseases through the use of germ-killing chemical formulations is not the curative approach in disease management. The true curative approach is provided by Ayurveda which shows the right way to cure by balancing the three humours of the body—phlegm, bile and wind.

Ayurveda tells us that if a disease is the result of morbid accumulation of phlegm in the human body, it brings harmful bacteria which outnumber the useful bacteria and produce painful symptoms of the disease. The solution is not in killing the harmful bacteria by antibiotics but lies in reducing the excessive phlegm in the body by eliminating it through natural purging process helped by herbs. The same holds good for diseases caused by excess of bile or wind humours in the body. No wonder, the sole focus on management of diseases considered infectious by administering antibiotics is leading to newer strains of harmful bacteria that are resistant to those antibiotics.

Automobile engineers and manufacturers made the entire global community freely run cars and trucks on octane till concerns over global warming caused by hydrocarbon emissions came to the fore. The wide use of chemical-based crop pesticides, food preservatives, food-colouring agents and also emulsifying and stabilizing agents has been insidiously inflicting damage to human tissues and it is now established that this use is one of the factors responsible for the huge incidence of cancer in recent times.

In the above examples, humans had knowledge gaps.

True knowledge is like the magic potion that refines human karma for sure-shot success. It is like the catalyst that hastens a chemical reaction to form the desired product to perfection. The yoga of knowledge is the application of true knowledge in human life.

Chapter 29

Self-help

Uddharey datmana atmanam, naatmaanvasadayeta,
Aatmayieva hyaatmano vasundharaatmayeva ripuraatmana.

Shri Krishna: *The self or soul is the vehicle for one's progress as well as downfall. So, through the power of the soul, elevate yourself and never let yourself fall from grace. The self or soul is one's greatest friend and also one's greatest enemy.*

The above verse delivered by Shri Krishna gives an exposition of the entire philosophy of human progress. It is a masterstroke statement.

You are your own guide. You are your own friend. You are your own foe. You are your own support. You are your own master. You can take yourself to the pinnacle of progress. You can let yourself fall to the abyss of unseemly existence. You are free to acquire sublime knowledge, which is fully and easily accessible to you. You are free to act according to that progress-enhancing knowledge. You are also free to violate the tenets of that knowledge and suffer the baneful consequences. You are floating in an infinite sea of super-spiritual element which possesses all knowledge and is all powerful. That element—

the almighty Creator—is your preceptor, guiding light and benefactor. He is constantly watching you and giving you guiding signals to facilitate your progress.

Nothing stands between you and your sublime goals—material or spiritual—except your own self. God helps those who help themselves. So self-help is the best help there can be.

The human soul is an inexhaustible source of energy. It energizes a human body for its lifetime of a hundred odd years and then enters another body and keeps it energized for another lifetime. This process goes on for thousands and millions of lifetimes. Imagine its potential. The power of the self, combined with right knowledge, is the total recipe for success in every human endeavour. Right knowledge is accessible through our inherent wisdom and is sourced to God. Meditation upon Him makes us receptive to his guiding signals which wean us away from wrongdoing. Whenever we are about to blunder, we experience pangs of fear, doubt or shame. These signals of fear, doubt or shame come from God. It is up to us to heed them or ignore them.

In one lifetime, we can persistently polish ourselves and progress to perfection. That is the power of the self. Realize it and move on. Nothing can deter a determined self from achieving its noble objectives. Powers permeating the universe help in realization of our dreams if only we are determined to go after them. God is perennially in a helping mode.

Man is, indeed, his own liberator.

It is a great irony that even in the twenty-first century of microcomputers and nanotechnology, the human being is hostage to scores of superstitions. More than half the world population believes in astrology and follows the guidance provided by astrologers and soothsayers in life. There can be nothing more damaging and detrimental to human progress than going by the advice of fortune tellers. There exist other types of superstitious practices, too, in the form of rituals. This verse of the Bhagwadgita has a message for such gullible humans who are entangled in superstitious practices. They must shed their belief in astrology and other irrational rituals and, instead, start believing in the power of the self. Realizing the enormous potential of the self and the power of perseverance, they will understand that there is no mundane goal that cannot be achieved through well-directed efforts.

The Buddhist school of thought harps on elevation of the self. It shows the philosophy of emancipation of the self through right knowledge and right action. Its practice provides a living proof of how faith and practice become the instruments of human deliverance. Its philosophy and adherence show the power of the self which has seen millions overcoming the challenges of life and rising to sublime levels. Careful deliberation upon the message of this verse convinces a person that God helps a person succeed in his endeavours by arming him, strengthening him and motivating him. Man is the architect of his own destiny and God is the prime facilitator of human achievements.

Applying the divine message of this verse to his life, the contemporary human can achieve all his worldly objectives through sheer willpower and faith. This message is the greatest human confidence booster there can ever be. Perhaps it is the most powerful motivator. Once a person understands the subtle meaning of this verse, he will boldly carve out his own way forward in life. Nothing will dampen his spirit. He will be holding the master key to success.

Chapter 30

Elevating the Self

Yogi yunjeet satatmaatmaanam rahasi sthita,
Aikaaki yatachittatma nirasheerparigraha.

Shri Krishna: *The yogi, living in seclusion as a hermit, away from the distractions of worldly life, in a self-dependent mode, should endeavour to establish communion with God. This is the way to elevating the self.*

A person who cuts himself off from the world, completely ceasing congress with others and lives a completely self-dependent life, comes nearer to God. His mind is not distracted from his prime objective, which is realization of the supreme divinity. Elevating the self needs a regimen of disciplined life. The human being is inherently frail because of his excitable and ever-wandering mind. The mind has to be bridled. This bridling of the mind is difficult in an environment with a lot of worldly distractions. Hence arises the need to move away to a secluded place, free of such distractions.

Mind is the medium of all actions performed by a human being. The elevation of the self can occur only through right knowledge and regulation of the mind. Through the mind, the person seeks gratification of the senses. This is his innate tendency. The more a person exposes himself to the attractions of the outside world, the more is the possibility of the mind going astray and succumbing to the desire of sensual gratification. Through the eyes, he seeks to behold glamorous objects. Through the ears, he wants to hear slanderous talk. Through his mouth, he desires to pander to his taste buds and indulge in eating and drinking immoderately and indiscriminately, without regard to unhealthy or healthy stuff. Thus, shutting the mind to the window of allurements of the outside world prepares a proper ground for meditation upon the Almighty and the consequent elevation of the self.

What is self-dependence? It is the cessation of all interaction with other humans for daily existence. When a person interacts with others in a give-and-take setting, he creates a compulsive situation of mutual expectation. This tends to erode mental peace, making the person restless. In such a situation, it is difficult to elevate the self. That explains the importance of occasional aloofness for spiritual refinement.

Even if the mind be under full control of the self, one needs right knowledge to proceed in the proper direction. Mental faculty and the motive energy need to be channelized in the right direction to achieve beneficial results.

Man is the master of his own destiny. Man depresses himself and only he elevates himself. The human self regresses when it gets disconnected from God, and it progresses when it gets connected. The power of the self is the power of the soul, which is a perennial source of energy. Therefore, believe in your own self to achieve all that you aspire for in life. Nothing is beyond your reach. Nothing can come between a determined self and its coveted noble object. Elevate yourself and go grab it.

Taking cue from the message contained in this verse, we

need to tap the power of silence and the power of solitude. The soul and the super-soul need to be exclusively together for the former to tap the latter's life-elevating and immortalizing nectar. We should visit natural bucolic spots, far away from the maddening crowds of cities. Watching the golden spread out across the azure sky in the eastern horizon during sunrise or the white cranes fishing in the virgin waters of a lake or a swarm of eagles gliding over a hillock in a balmy evening would make us feel God's power and presence. Living in such surroundings and practising yogic meditation help to establish communion with God. We have to do this and actually experience this. That will be a real life-elevating experience.

Silent contemplation will help the human to look inwards and that alone can give many answers to the problems being faced by him. Silence is extremely powerful in its own way because it provides the soul and the superpowerful universal soul to come together through the medium of the human mind and intellect.

Today's life is built and revolves around cities. These urban centres have become the hubs of capitalist institutions, like factories, commercial plazas and banks, and harbour huge human habitations where transported natural resources are heavily concentrated and used by large hordes of populations. The natural spread and dispersal of these resources is heavily disturbed. Thus occurs the destruction of natural ambience of the global regions that get converted into congested urban centres, marked by concrete jungles. We find neither serenity nor seclusion there. Perhaps we need to relook at modern human habitations. We need to build the ambience of our dwelling areas in a way that takes us closer to nature and the Creator.

Chapter 31

The Yogic Pose

Samankaya shirogreevam dhaarayanna chalam sthirah,
Samprekshaya naasikaagram swam dishashchanvalokayanan,
Yatha deep niwatastho negantey sopama smrita.

Shri Krishna: *The yogi should sit in a straight posture, with the body and neck erect. The body should be kept still and the yogi, without looking in any other direction, should focus his attention on his nostrils and at the same time chant the name of God (the syllable 'Aum'). He should keep his body as still as a lighted lamp with its wick burning in still air.*

The body posture has a lot to do with the mind. The mind is the driver of all senses which include the five cognitive senses of touch, taste, smell, hearing and sight and the five physical senses which exist in the form of action organs—feet, anus, genitals, hands and tongue. Through these ten senses, a human being performs all worldly karmas. But the mind being the driver of these senses, actions originate in the mind. Therefore, the key to performance of right actions is regulation of the excitable and often uncontrollable mind.

How exactly does the mind drive the senses? It is through the primordial element of air. The nerves in the body are the channels of air and it is the mind which controls the flow of this vital element of air through these channels for the working of senses and the sensory organs as aforesaid. The mind has to be kept in control to maintain its composure and stability.

Keeping the body posture erect helps in maintaining mental composure and stability. In scientific terms, this happens by maintaining the balance of the air element in the body. This can be better understood by citing the case of diseases in the human body which carry nagging symptoms of pain in external organs and we undergo treatments like physiotherapy, acupressure or acupuncture for treatment of these diseases. What do these treatments do? They release excess of air element in those organs, thus alleviating the symptoms of pain. Pain is caused by excessive accumulation of air in a body organ. And bad posturing is an established cause of many body ailments that carry symptoms of pain in organs like neck, shoulders, arms, ankles or hips.

Shri Krishna was the master of the Vedas that incorporate the divine science of Ayurveda, which provides complete understanding of cause and cure of all human diseases. Therefore, keeping the spine erect is basic to yoga of the body and mind, and Shri Krishna has emphasized precisely on this.

The yogic posture of sitting erect needs to be properly practised by a yoga aspirant. In this posture, chanting of the divine syllable, Aum, helps to connect with the infinite pool of the superior spiritual element called God, from whom flows divine energy to the human organism. It purges the human mind of its banal elements and this purification of the mind further aids in its regulation.

Modern medical science also recognizes the fact that keeping the spine erect is crucial to maintenance of good health of the entire nervous system. In the erect posture, positive energy flows through the human body and mind. Persons who do not keep their posture erect become hosts to a variety of ailments, like spondylosis and various types of chronic aches and pains. Mental health of a person has a direct correlation with the posture. Persons with wrong posture are prone to anxiety, depression and schizophrenia.

A healthy mind can exist only inside a healthy body. Good mental health is fundamental to yogic practice. Good mental health is also the prime requisite to spiritual development of the human being.

No amount of games or sports activity or sessions in the gymnasium can serve to improve the health of the human spine than the regimen of classical yogic practice. The bending and stretching exercises of yoga quite significantly help in achieving the straightness of the spine which results in an erect posture. One has to experience this by actually doing it. The outcome of regular yogic exercise is immediately palpable. You lose anxiety, fear and depression and gain on cheerfulness and mental composure.

The global popularity of yoga, understood as a regimen of physical exercises, has gained tremendously in recent years. This is testified by the recognition of 21 June as International Yoga Day, at the call and behest of the Prime Minister of India in 2016. Modern medical fraternity recognizes yoga as a potent technique for effective management of a host of ailments, like heart disease, obesity and mental depression. Meditation is now officially recognized as a mode of treatment in mental ailments. Posturing of the body in yoga is the basic element in this.

Chapter 32

We are All Alike

Aatmaupamyein sarvatra samam pashyatiyo Arjun,
Sukham va yadi va dukham sa yogi paramo matah.

Shri Krishna: O Arjun, a person who sees and believes that other persons are like him in happy or unhappy states or in joy and suffering, such a person is a super yogi.

We are all sailing in the same boat. We are birds of the same feather, flocked together. We are all alike in frailties and strengths, in happy or unhappy experiences of life. A person who has understood this reality perceives others like him—happy or unhappy, weak in some areas and strong in others, undergoing high and low phases in life. Such a person has understood the true nature of the soul.

The soul, according to the Vedas, is characterized by the inherent attributes of desire, passion, likes, dislikes, perseverance, happiness, sadness, wisdom, foolishness and cognition. Therefore, all human beings share these characteristics. This shows how similar all human beings are in thoughts, tendencies and actions. The reason for this is quite simple. They all are seeking the same goal of salvation. The roadblocks to that goal are the same, created by the innate forces of desire, passion or imprudence. The mechanism of human spiritual elevation is a standard mechanism, set by the Creator.

If you are hurt by certain actions or remarks of others and you are aware that others are like you in this respect, you will refrain from indulging in such actions or remarks in your dealings. Other persons' acts of compassion, sympathy and charity make you happy. Realizing this fact will make you sympathetic, charitable and compassionate too. Do unto others as you would have them do unto you.

Responses in human interactions are naturally reciprocal. Kindness begets kindness. Love begets love. Hatred begets hatred. Politeness begets politeness. You get back what you give to others. Hence, your mental perspective should be such as to radiate warmth and affection around.

A great message emanates from this verse.

You should always be eager to extend that helping hand to others. You will get the same in return. Spread positivity, and positive vibes will come back at you. This simple fact of life provides you the mantra for happiness and success in life and for your spiritual elevation, which will take you closer to your ultimate goal of moksha.

The universe returns to you what you give to it.

The very belief that others are like you will iron out many differences and disputes between you and others. With such belief, zones of understanding between humans will overlap rather than remain apart.

It is strange that today the whole world is connected through the Internet and mobile telephony and yet differences in thoughts, thought processes, ideologies and perceptions of humans dispersed across the globe have not significantly thinned down. Technology has not helped to reduce markedly the cultural divides between humans. The present world also presents a picture of nations at loggerheads with each other and of communities afflicted with racial prejudice and ethnocentrism. The understanding that all persons have common hopes, aspirations and goals and are engaged in struggles to reach those goals is something that has the potential to bridge the ideological divides between global humans. It can bring people closer and make the world a true global village. It can greatly help to increase economic and cultural cooperation between nations in a mutually beneficial manner.

At the individual level, the feeling that all human beings are cast in the same mould in terms of basic needs, hopes, desires and objectives can improve human relationships in a tremendous way. This perspective is bound to make a person see the other's point of view in an interaction. This will make him more empathetic. It will bring down squabbles and disputes. It will set in motion winds of harmony where differences and discords exist.

It is not difficult for most people to understand and appreciate the fact that many of the human interaction and relationship problems spring from misunderstanding, doubt and suspicion. Human thinking is often very irrational, very flawed. It is so because persons are unable to appreciate others' points of view as they have no idea of others' problems and situations. If a person begins to think from another person's standpoint, he can always understand the other person better. He will empathize with him and strike a collaborative and cooperative note with him.

If you understand that others are like you, you will be patient, empathetic and level-headed in your approach. Then where is the doubt that you will be a better human being, facilitating your own and others' spiritual development all the way?

Chapter 33

The Power of Divine Connection

Yo ma pashyati sarvatra cha mayi pashyati,
Tasyaham na pranashyaami sa cha mey na pranashyati.

Shri Krishna: *If a person sees the creator, God, everywhere and also sees everything in God, he never falls from divine grace and never gets distanced from God.*

God, as an infinite spiritual substance, pervades the entire universe. This is the terse way to explain his omnipresence. At the same time, this spiritual substance is subtler than inanimate matter and living souls. Therefore, in scientific terms, all material objects of the universe and all human souls are contained in Him. This is the most fundamental metaphysical fact that a human being should understand. With such understanding settled at the back of his mind, he will always remain alive to the realities of life and conscious of the significance of his connection with the supreme divinity. He will, accordingly, perform all actions with the understanding that God is constantly watching him, always with him and beside him with His guidance and beneficence.

With this awareness always in an individual's mind that he is ever swimming in an infinite sea of spirituality, his thoughts and actions will be in sync with this divine truth and, therefore, progressive. He will treat happiness and sadness alike. He will look at success and failure as two sides of the same coin. He will breathe, eat, sleep and work thinking about his real goal of salvation. His mundane shortsightedness will be replaced by a divine farsightedness.

One can never get distanced from God in physical terms. But yes, one can get distanced from Him in metaphysical terms. If an individual stops being conscious of the ultimate reality, he will remain in the labyrinth of the material world, struggling and stuttering in the fulfilment of his desires, exulting in success and depressed in failure, tending to put the blame on others for his failures and falling prey to the frailties of greed and anger. These will choke his development.

Divine grace of the Almighty is always available for each one of us. It is really upto us to remain mentally connected with Him by being ever-conscious of His overwhelming omnipresence and constant support in our life. The power of divine connection is of an uplifting and delivering nature—refining our characters and facilitating our emancipation from the multiple miseries of worldly life.

Animal living is an existence. Human living is an art. Humans have to understand and carefully navigate through the life course. They have to learn and unlearn things. They fall, rise and fall again only to rise higher than before. This is the beauty of human living. This beauty comes from the understanding of the divine connection. It is easy for some people to say and equally easy for others to believe that no entity like God exists and the entire world came on its own and keeps changing on its own. But even today, a far greater majority of global population is a believer. The belief may be based on understanding or faith. But the benefits of leading a life with a conscious connection with the divine Creator are better experienced than described in words. One human experience based on faith further reinforces this faith. This in itself is a most exciting tale of spiritual development.

Man's divine connection with God is based on his relationship with Him. This relationship, in turn, is based on desires of both. It is premised on human limitations set against God's infinite capacity to instruct, guide, direct, control and deliver. Human desires are more material and less spiritual. God's desires are all spiritual—to maintain order, peace, harmony in the universe and enable humans to realize their potential progressively and reach their goals of salvation. The two are eternally together as parent-child, master-servant, preceptor-pupil and ruler-ruled. Their relationship is all-encompassing, comprehensive and complete. It leaves no gaps that may hamper or pause or slow down human progress.

In view of the above, it is not difficult for today's scientific and rational-minded human to establish a connection with his Creator after understanding the importance of faith.

It is also possible to see in this context that God consciousness on the part of modern man is bound to give him positivity which will manifest in a remarkably healthy and positive attitude to things around him. Positivity will generate hope and confidence. It will quell fear, doubt and scepticism. It will bring him in sync with the natural flow of circumstances orchestrated by the Master of the universe. It will make him collaborate with the good and virtuous and confront the evil and vicious.

Divine connection as a term appears to be esoteric. But it is a facet of our core reality of existence. We need to be always aware of the power of divine link with the Almighty. If we perform our daily, worldly tasks with this awareness in our conscious and subconscious minds, nothing can obstruct our progressive ascent in life.

Chapter 34

The Primordial Elements of the Almighty

Bhumirapo analo vayu kham mano buddhireva cha,
Ahankaar itiyam mey bhinna prakritirashtatha,
Aham kritsnasya jagatah prabhavah pralayasthaa.

Shri Krishna: *God creates the entire universe through eight material elements. These different elements are earth, water, fire, air, ether, mind, intellect and ego. He works through these very elements to bring about dissolution of the universe.*

Shri Krishna was a complete scholar of the Vedas, and in some of his small verses, he has wonderfully encapsulated the divine wisdom of many hymns of the Vedas. Modern scientists have understood many aspects of material nature but they are yet far away from unravelling many more mysteries of the universe. Let alone the universe, they have not been able to understand many things about this earth, including its tectonic changes, the human mind and even the human and animal body. They have no sure ideas about the time of origin of life on this planet or the age of the earth. Even today, many pieces of their understanding are conjectural. They are yet to be substantiated and verified.

Modern scientists have discovered atoms, molecules,

electrons, protons, neutrons and positrons. They state that subatomic particles are the building blocks of matter. But they have no clear clue as to how life originated. What exactly is the difference between animate and inanimate entities on this earth? Does human, animal and plant life exist on other planets of our solar system and elsewhere in the vast universe? Is there any tangible entity as a living soul? If so, what are its characteristics? Is there any tangible entity as the intelligent creator and controller of the universe? There are no clear answers to these questions.

To get answers to the aforesaid questions, we need to look at material nature through the prism of the Vedas, which reveal that all inanimate or lifeless matter is made of five basic elements—earth, fire, water, air and ether. The mind, intellect and ego of living beings were also carved out of these basic elements. The animate entities existing in the universe, viz. the living souls and God, were never created. They are eternal.

Arguably the greatest scientist of our time, Albert Einstein, believed there exists a supernatural, super-intelligent creator. He also believed that such a creator works and operates scientifically. But, at the same time, he believed that our existing knowledge of science is still in its infancy. We have to go far to unravel the mysteries of nature and its creator. Einstein is remembered for the famous quote, 'Science without religion is lame. Religion without science is blind.'

Religion, as understood in common parlance, and science are complementary to each other. Through a systematic understanding of the primordial five elements of nature, one derives a sound concept of the creation of universe and also a sound understanding of the Creator.

Subtle understanding and application of the eight primordial elements of nature will give us a deeper insight into the various aspects of nature. It will raise our science and technology to higher and further higher levels. Yes, through such application, we shall be able to construct environment-friendly space vehicles for travel to distant worlds inhabited by humans, probably like us. Knowledge of ether and its scientific application would lend to development of such vehicles which could travel at the speed of light, i.e. 300,000 km per second.

Through application of the knowledge of primal elements to human body, we shall be able to understand its functioning in a far better way. We can then dramatically raise our standards of health and longevity. It is documented in the epic Mahabharat, that Bhishma died at the age of 175 years and Shri Krishna lived for 125 years.

At the individual level, knowledge of the eight primordial elements will help us to comprehensively understand our body, mind, intellect and soul, and the ways these are connected and interrelated. Our progress path will be better laid out. We shall lead far happier and better quality lives. Today's humans have little knowledge of these primal elements and human race, though claiming to be scientifically advanced, it is still groping in the dark in many fields.

Metaphysics and spirituality are higher sciences. We are yet far away from a thorough comprehension of them. We shall do well if we undertake dedicated research in these areas to solve the pressing problems of the day and to achieve quantum progress in all spheres of human life.

Chapter 35

The Primary Cause and Basis of All

Mattah parataram naanyat kimchidasti dhananjaya,
Mayi sarvamidam proktam; sutre maniganaa iva.

Shri Krishna: O Dhananjaya, God declares that He is the greatest of all and above everything. He pervades all things and is the basic building force behind everything. He holds together all constituent particles of matter like beads threaded together in a necklace.

This most fundamental fact needs to be realized by every human being. Since God is a spirit, he is not subject to laws of material nature. He is beyond the laws of physics and chemistry. He does not consist of electrons, protons, neutrons, positrons or photons. He is a spiritual substance beyond time and space. He is beyond physical dimensions. He has boundless power. That power makes him omnipotent. There exist eternal particles of primordial physical matter in the universe. God works upon them, and through His power and infinite intelligence, creates the celestial space called ether and thereafter the constellations, galaxies, suns, planets and moons at the onset of creation. Many of these celestial objects form the abodes of living souls, who are eternal too.

The constituent particles of matter were in an inert state before the creation of universe. God provided that negative charge to the electron and positive charge to the proton. His power holds the electrons in an orbital motion around the nucleus of every atom. The force of gravity is also a manifestation of His giant power. The kaleidoscopic beauty of matter in its various forms and shades eloquently expresses the power of the almighty Creator. Look at the millions of species of plants and animals inhabiting this earth. The huge variety of bodies of birds, reptiles, amphibians, mammals, plants, shrubs, trees and insects is a vivid testimony to His infinite intelligence and power.

Imagine water, the fluid that sustains all life on our planet earth. Eighteen milliliters of water contain 602,300,000,000,000,000,000,000 molecules, all held together through some bonding force, which is due to the power of God. In a similar way, the bonding force of all constituent particles of matter in its wonderful variegated shades comes from the same Creator. He is the primary cause and the fundamental basis of all and everything in this visible universe.

A true scientist understands matter and is also able to understand God who created the universe out of basic matter. Knowledge of matter is half knowledge and knowledge of matter, Creator and souls, alongwith their relationship, is full and complete knowledge. To understand cause, you need to understand effect. God being the cause of everything is at once comprehensible through a systematic understanding of the material universe and the mode of its functioning.

This verse provides a sound conceptual idea of God, who is conveyed as all-powerful and all-pervasive at the same time. Working subtly, He is able to exercise complete control over all matter. This clear concept strengthens and accentuates human faith in that supernatural entity.

What does man need to fear and worry about when he has that infinite pool of knowledge, wisdom, power and benevolence beside him at all times? Understanding reinforces belief, and belief in the Almighty equips humankind for action, success and progress. Surrendering to Him wipes out his doubts and fear and brings him in alignment with truth and reality. It becomes the panacea for all the ills and all the troubles afflicting him.

Comprehension of the expanse, power and control of the almighty God gives a person the right frame of mind for proper action that inevitably brings success and happiness. This happens through reinforcement of faith in that supreme divine power, as indicated above. Modern world is witness to a marked dilution of this faith.

Self-proclaimed rationalists decry the existence of a universal power that controls things. Their arguments seem to be logical up to a certain point but not beyond it. The concept of the Creator that provides the binding force to subatomic particles, while at the same time existing all over the ethereal space, is at once comprehensible. Hence, this verse of the Bhagwadgita builds up faith based on knowledge and understanding. Such a faith is steadfast and not blind, because it is not built on superstition or half knowledge. Blind faith has been the bane of human society for ages, as it has generated religious bigotry and led to so much bloodshed in the name of religion. Modern man needs to embrace this scientific concept of the Creator. This will keep him connected with Him. And that connection is the contrivance for human deliverance.

Chapter 36

Core and Crux

Rasoahamapsu kaunteya! Prabhasmi shashisuryayo,
Pranavah sarvavedeshu shabdakhey paurusham nrishu.

Shri Krishna: *God declares, 'I exist in water as fluid. In moonlight and sunlight, I exist as rays of energy. I am the worthy syllable 'Aum' in the Vedas. In the vast ethereal space, I manifest as the reverberating word. In humans, I show myself as the power of perseverance.'*

In this verse, Shri Krishna conveys to Arjun in first person what God has conveyed to humankind through the Vedas. He is at the core of all matter visible in the universe. He is the crux of all phenomena—terrestrial or celestial—that we see around us. He is truly the core and crux of everything.

What gives water its viscous nature?

The answer is—its molecular structure and intermolecular spacing.

Who created this typical structure and spacing?

None other than the almighty God.

Both sunlight and moonlight are a flow of particles called photons, as discovered by modern scientists. Are the photons fundamental and indivisible particles of matter? Scientists believe that they are not. The Vedas reveal that all particles that build various objects were carved out of primordial matter which existed in a fluid state. Who carved out these particles? The one and only Creator, benefactor and regulator.

The Vedas are the original words of the creator, God. His prime name is Aum with which he is identified and addressed in the Vedas. Depending upon his multiple attributes and non-attributes, he can be identified with countless names. But Aum remains his prime name, which is why this name appears all over the hymns of the Vedas.

The vast material entity called ether was also created by God. We can hear sound of words when they travel in space. We get the concept and perception of ether through these words. The reverberating sound of words reminds us of His existence.

The power of perseverance in human beings comes through consciousness and knowledge. Consciousness is innate in the human soul but knowledge comes from God. That is why human efforts for any progressive cause are ascribed to the Creator, who gave all knowledge to his human subjects.

Modern human life has become distanced from God. The reasons are not far to seek. God consciousness has waned. To live well and get the best out of our precious lives, we humans need to be conscious of the Creator at all times. We should never forget Him in the daily grind of our mundane existence. And more importantly, we need to follow the injunctions of the Vedas all the times. Whenever we are in confusion or dilemma, we can look into the Vedas for answers and we will not be disappointed. The Vedas are the eternal books of guidance for humanity. If we follow the message of the Vedas in letter and spirit, our material, as well as spiritual, accomplishments can rise manifold.

Being always conscious of the Creator in daily life will keep today's humans well in touch with reality. Talking of water or when I am drinking water, I am reminded of God who created this element for human consumption and sustenance. When I think so, I am also reminded that I should use this substance moderately and prudently. I should not waste it nor splurge it. I should not be polluting it. I should be following the practice of water management as prescribed in the Vedas, so that the global distribution and quality of this vital substance is not disturbed. What is happening in many regions of the world today is quite different.

The value of air as an element is borne out by similar considerations. Air pollution is a colossal global problem today whose rectification is a big challenge for the contemporary civilization.

Perseverance is the bedrock of progress of a human being. But not everybody can work hard and for long hours. The distractions are many and the mind is frail. Being conscious of the fact that the power of human perseverance too is a gift of the Almighty will keep us in touch with God through faith and worship, and we shall be able to work our way to every desired success more easily.

God consciousness has nothing to do with any labelled traditional religion. But it has everything to do with human existence and human happiness. The sooner today's humans realize it, the better it will be.

When human beings begin to understand God as the be-all and end-all of everything, they start seeing life in its true perspective. They become conscious of the fundamental realities of existence and, consequently, well-tracked for progress. The meaning and import of this verse of the Bhagwadgita, if applied to our life, will make it better aligned with truth and the core reality permeating the universe.

Chapter 37

Modes of Manifestation

Punyo gandhah prithivyam cha tejashchasmi vibhavasau,
Jeevanam sarvabhuteshu tapashchasmi tapasvishu.

Shri Krishna (on behalf of God): *I am the fragrance in the earth, effulgence in the fire. I am manifesting as the life in all living beings and penance in the ascetics.*

God is not an enigma or mystery. He is the most obvious living reality. A mere logical approach to seeing everything makes a person understand God, who is the essence in all things. A human being is well familiar with fragrances in various substances. This fragrance is attributed to the specific properties of substances and the sensory power of humans who perceive it. Both are the creations of God. The specific physical and chemical properties of a substance which include its unique molecular structure are designed and set by God. Likewise, the sense of smell provided to living organisms is also created by God through primordial matter.

The heat and brilliance of fire is the energy which is a manifestation of the creator God who released this energy of the primordial matter which was in an inert state before the onset of creation. The brilliance in fire is due to Him. The warmth in the sunlight is because of Him.

Life in its visible forms is ascribed to God, who provided body, senses, mind and intellect to the eternal living soul. The living soul is so small that it is invisible to the naked eye. Its existence cannot be captured even by the most powerful electronic microscope because it lacks particulate character and is spiritual in nature. That fish swimming in the pond, that ant crawling on the ground, that eagle gliding through the sky, that cactus growing in the desert, that frog hopping on the soil and that monkey jumping through the trees are all living souls in essence. They are visible because they possess physical bodies given to them by the Creator.

The ascetics perform hard penance in a secluded existence because they have realized their ultimate goals as human beings. This realization and the consequent actions involving transcendental techniques of physical and mental regulation are prompted by God dwelling within their minds. He enlightens them to their true goals, facilitating their journey all the way.

God manifests himself through innumerable modes. His human subjects have to possess the right mental framework to understand and appreciate the manifestations of the Creator. This framework is built upon a correct understanding of basic metaphysical facts and a logical perspective. Such a perspective and understanding will transform an agnostic or atheist into a theist, giving a more progressive orientation to his life. To the ordinary human being, it will provide a deeper insight into the problems and processes of life, making him better equipped to deal with all issues and steer his life boat with fulfilment and success in the journey.

The average man of modern times knows that all matter is made of atoms and molecules. Most people also know that the red tinge of the rose, the tallness of the steeple, the viscosity of water, the bitterness of quinine, the sweetness of jaggery or the blackness of coal are due to various combinations and structures of atoms and molecules. When a person understands that all these combinations and structures are created by God, he begins to comprehend Him. He realizes that God is a subtle, all-pervasive entity that operates at the micro levels. When the average educated individual of modern age further understands that various forms of energy like light, heat and ionizing radiation, like X-rays and gamma rays, are the play of subatomic particles which are the creations of God, he acquires a better comprehension of God. Nothing supports this statement more than the fact that in recent times, scientists working with nanotechnology have discovered a micro-sized energy-packed particle, which they have termed 'God particle'.

Drawing upon the message of this verse, man will understand that human mind is also derived from primal matter and the process behind this is driven by the all-powerful God. Based on this, man will acquire a true, scientific understanding of his own mind, the driver of his every action. Equipped with the subtle knowledge of mind and intellect, man can undoubtedly put his natural faculties to better use for his own happiness and satisfaction. Better understanding of the self will further refine the understanding of the Creator. Better knowledge of the human faculties will, no doubt, lend themselves to their optimal utilization.

Today's human being is more constrained by the under-utilization of his own inherent faculties than anything else. It is a great irony. With deeper and sharper understanding of body, mind and intellect, man will be able to put them all to far greater utilization. And this will enable him to accomplish more in life.

If you know yourself and your Creator well, you can get what you want.

Chapter 38

The Essence of Everything

Buddhirbuddhi matasmasmi tejastey jasvinaamaham,
Balam balavataam chaham kaamraagvivirjitam.

Shri Krishna (on behalf of God): *I am the intellect of the intellectuals; the brilliance of the brilliant. I am also the strength of the strong, devoid of passion.*

As has been stated in the previous chapters, God is the cause of all and everything. He is all-pervasive. He has created everything in the universe except the living souls which were never created, being eternal and indestructible. Hence, he is also the creator of human intellect that was carved out of matter. When I am applying my intellect to understand and articulate any subject, I am using the power of my creator God. Akin to the computers in wide use today, the hardware in our body in the form of brain and software in the form of mind and intellect are used for all thought processes. Both the hardware and the software are the handiwork of God.

A spiritually enlightened person radiates brilliance. This brilliance is the result of his spiritual elevation through the transcendental techniques of yoga. Where does the knowledge of yoga come from? It comes from the same Creator, revealed in the Vedas. Man applies this knowledge to uplift himself using his physical body, mind and intellect, all of which were provided to him by God. Then where is the doubt that human brilliance is the brilliance of his Creator?

The human soul is power. The human strength, which is physical, mental and intellectual in nature, shows up through the appurtenances of the soul—the body, mind and intellect—which are given by the Creator. This strength can be moral or immoral. It can be righteous or unrighteous. It can be selfish or selfless. It can be passionate or without the element of passion. Strength without passion produces well-directed action; impassioned strength can make a person go overboard or berserk in his actions. Strength without passionate attachment is beneficent strength which is divine, not human. It is ascribed to the Creator of man. In the exercise of such strength, a human being protects the weak and fights the wicked persons. His actions promote peace and progress in the community.

God is really at the core of every harmonizing attribute, static or dynamic, that we observe in living organisms and lifeless objects existing in the universe. He represents the pure, unadulterated water in the sea, rivers, oceans, ponds and lakes. He is represented by the coolness and soothing attribute of moonlight and also the warmth and vitalizing quality of sunlight. Everything that is strong, pure, orderly, elevating, harmonizing and progressive represents Him because these qualities are similar to His attributes. The Master of the universe is also the cause and basis of everything contained in the universe.

Understanding the Creator through a comprehension of the core attributes of living and non-living entities in the world would reinforce human faith in Him. At the same time, it will make humans better aware of their relationship with the Creator.

Modern humans will do well to acquire this understanding. This will make them more rational in their outlook. At the same time, such understanding is bound to unite humanity based on commonality of thought and ideology.

An intellectually gifted person is an asset to his community and society. We have heard and read about intellectual giants who had a measured intelligence quotient (IQ) of over 150. Some of these were outstanding writers and philosophers, others were scientists and yet others, grandmasters at chess. A person who is intellectually gifted should link his intellectual prowess to his creator, God. By doing so, he will not develop pride and arrogance and will be spared of the deleterious consequences thereof. As long as he remains humble, he will be able to exploit his high capability well. The same is true in the context of other human qualities, like physical strength and stamina.

Muhammad Ali, the champion heavyweight boxer, remained a devout Muslim after conversion. He displayed a steady and strong faith. This was probably his greatest strength.

We owe it to Him for what we are and what we accomplish and what we become on the basis of our accomplishments. Affluence, power, fame, glory are truly not ours, though they appear to be so. We have to credit it all to the Creator whose eternal knowledge and power makes it possible for us humans to achieve small, incremental feats in life.

Today, we hear that modern technology and scientific implements like computers, Internet and mobile telephony have transformed the world into a global village. But this is a virtual village, based on virtual world of the Internet. Differing ideologies and philosophies have perpetuated the distances between minds and hearts of global humans. The understanding of God through this verse would narrow down these distances and make the world a true global village.

Chapter 39

Who Worships Him?

Chaturvidha bhajantey maam janaa sukritino Arjun,
Sarto jigyasurtharthi gyani cha bharatarshabh,
Vasudevah sarvamii sa mahatma sudurlabhah.

Shri Krishna: O Arjun, God says that four types of persons worship Him. They are categorized as 1) one who is in a miserable condition 2) a curious knowledge seeker 3) one with unfulfilled desires and 4) the erudite and enlightened one. Who is the greatest among them? The enlightened one who understands God as the all-pervasive superior spirit.

Truly, these four types of people worship God. An old saying goes that there would be no God if it was not necessary to invent Him. Since God is an esoteric subject or object, the common man seeks God only for serving his worldly necessity.

But men are of various types and grades. The ordinary man seeks God's helping hand when he is distressed, in bailing him out of his miserable situation. The more refined or matured individual who is inquisitive, worships Him because he believes that God is omniscient and the source of all knowledge. The third category is that of persons with unfulfilled desires. Human beings live with hundreds of desires. It is only these mundane desires that impel a person for action, that make him persevere. But in spite of striving and struggling in the pursuit of his goals, success often eludes him. Then he prays to the Almighty. This is natural, but only for the believer. The fourth category of worshippers is the erudite ones. They worship Him because they understand that worshipping is their most important action. They know well their eternal relationship with the Almighty and the power of worship for maintaining their bond with God and invoking His blessings.

Worship of God is natural for the average human being because he is powerless and clueless in negotiating the many hurdles that confront him through his life. He seeks the helping hand of his all-powerful and compassionate Master. He believes out of faith that his Master is his true friend, philosopher and guide, being his omniscient Creator.

Worship is an action that follows belief, faith and understanding. The average class of humans believes in the power of God, and their devotion is based on faith. The highest class human understands his eternal relationship with his Creator and also has a clear comprehension of His attributes. His devotion is transcendental. His desires are not material but spiritual. He knows that the ultimate purpose of life is salvation and he seeks the same in his worship. His faith is based on a crystal clear concept of his limitations, God's power and his relationship with God.

Worship brings humans near to God, that infinite pool of beneficent spiritual energy which is ever available for tapping. This nearness to God is not physical. Physically—measured in terms of distance in ethereal space—God is ever close to us. We are placed in his lap. The distance between God and his human subjects is mental. How we understand Him, perceive

Him and remain conscious of Him is what counts and what matters. The Creator knows, better than we do, what is good and what is bad for us, and therefore, we often do not realize why our problems do not go away. He wants us to solve our own problems and helps us in doing that. He helps us in our process of refinement which steers us to our ultimate goal of moksha.

Greatest among human worshippers of the Creator are those who regard Him omnipresent. With such an outlook, the worshipper will never seek bounties for himself in a selfish mode, for, he will always be conscious of the fact that the Creator, who exists everywhere, is bound to do full justice to all. Hence, the enlightened worshipper will always be selfless. That, in effect, is the sublime angle to worship.

The message emanating from this verse too has the potential of stemming superstition and obscurantism from the world. There is lot of falsehood and superstition existing in human society in the name of religion. People expect favours from God by performing rituals without working hard for their desired goals. People start performing prayers to invoke the blessings of God for bringing victory to their preferred candidates in competitive politics or sports, without realizing that the same God is also God to their candidates' competitors. Getting to know the true meaning, intent and effect of worship will make man perceive God with realism. It will make him more practical and realistic and reinforce the message that God helps those who help themselves. It will make the individual more industrious and perseverant. This verse also conveys that the supreme Creator, who is also the prime benefactor of humanity, expects his human subjects to develop a sound concept and comprehension of Him—for their own betterment, welfare and upliftment. Hence, humans need to understand God as the all-pervasive super-soul.

Understanding God as a superior, infinite soul will serve to rationalize many other concepts of global humans. It will make them realize that all living creatures inhabiting the universe are subjects of that one and only God. It will make them more compassionate, and broadminded too.

Chapter 40

The Support of the Almighty

Jaramaranamokshaya mamashritya yatanti ye,
Tey brahm tadwidu kritsna madhyatmam karm chaakhilam.

Shri Krishna (on behalf of God): *Those who endeavour to get themselves liberated from the miseries of old age and death by leaning on me; they are able to acquire all spiritual knowledge and fully understand the philosophy of karmas.*

A person who leans on God for support, gets gradually liberated from pain, privation and penury. He is able to fulfil his mundane desires and reach a stage where he has no remnant material desires. His desires become all sublime and spiritual. Then, he is able to prepare himself for his ultimate goal by getting unshackled from the bondage of cyclic death and rebirth. In the process of this preparation, he becomes progressively enlightened through acquisition of the knowledge of metaphysical truths and the spiritual laws that regulate life.

The support of the Almighty is a panacea for all human problems. This is an inviolable truth which is difficult to perceive by the common man but is understood by the spiritually refined person. Spiritual knowledge is the knowledge of the characteristics of the soul, characteristics of the larger, superior soul called God and their interrelationship. Man grows spiritually refined when he starts living as per the injunctions of the Vedas, the scriptures containing the direct message of the creator God for his human subjects. By following the message of these divine scriptures, he develops a clear understanding of the law of human action and reaction, of karmic retribution.

Leaning on God is a near metaphorical expression for getting help of the Almighty in all worldly affairs. Drawing upon Him for help has to be understood in spiritual terms. This process takes place through fixation of the mind, based on faith. Through this fixation of human mind on God for his support in all worldly tasks, man is able to enhance peace and harmony and enable better usage of his faculties. He does not get perturbed by problems. He takes challenges head on and successfully overcomes hurdles in life.

Treating God as your prime benefactor frees you of all your worries and tensions. This happens when you develop an unshakeable faith in His support. You then become more efficient, more productive and, obviously, more success-oriented. Fear does not grip you then. You start challenging the challenges that life throws at you. You move forward fast, clearing all the obstacles on the way with your own efforts. The support of the Almighty empowers you all the way. The experiences that you gain while negotiating your way through the jungle of adversities of life make you both knowledgeable and wise. The meaning of life is revealed to you in practical terms.

The support of the Almighty is freely available to all His human subjects. It only has to be tapped. To tap that support, one needs to understand its infinite expanse. One needs to understand and follow the right way or the correct procedure to do it.

How can modern man lean on God and improve his life? Modern psychologists and psychoanalysts talk a lot about the powers of the subconscious mind. It is the human subconscious mind that is the storehouse of all memories, knowledge and skills. Concepts, ideas and ideologies lie stored or buried in the subconscious mind. Complex phenomena, like intuition, telepathy, premonition and clairvoyance, also belong to the realm of the subconscious mind. Psychologists have, on record, stated that by tapping the enormous power of the subconscious mind, a human being can achieve great and remarkable feats. This has been the subject of practical demonstration also, which testifies to the latent power of the subconscious mind that can help a human to unleash his high potential in any endeavour. By leaning on God, a person can connect with Him through his subconscious mind. He then develops a latent sense of security which removes his fear in every mundane situation. It makes him feel sound and secure and emboldens him to attempt big tasks and succeed in them through the dint of his efforts. It is a great thing to be out of fear. Fear kills a man even before the arrival of death.

'Cowards die many times before their death. The valiant never taste of death but once'.*

If a person has conquered fear, he has entered the zone of invincibility.

A person does not know himself fully well. He hardly knows others' minds. Then how can he understand his mundane situations? It is but natural that he will be gripped by fear of the unknown. He will have that nagging sense of insecurity every now and then. Under such circumstances, faith in God and leaning on Him in all situations will remove his fear.

Julius Caesar, Act 2, Scene 2, William Shakespeare

Fear of the known or unknown and anger corrode human life. Faith in God and His subconscious support come useful exactly here. They have the power to kill both anger and fear. Peaceful state of human mind is the fertile ground for sustained and proper actions that bring sure-shot success to a person in every endeavour.

Chapter 41

The Last Moments

Antakaaley cha maamev smaranmuktwa klewaram,
Ya prayati sa maddhawam yaati naastyatra sanshaya.

Shri Krishna (on behalf of God): *He who remembers me during his dying moments, reaches my abode unquestionably.*

Faith in the Almighty makes us remember Him during times of distress, in the earnest hope that He will take care of all our problems and worries. Ordinary humans cannot understand how God works, how He responds and delivers us from our sorrows. Most of us do not tend to believe what we cannot see with our eyes, what we cannot hear with our ears, what we cannot touch, taste or smell, or otherwise perceive through our senses. With the development of science and technology and the invention of modern scientific implements, like radio telescope and electron microscope, we are able to see distant celestial objects, like stars, planets and comets, and also small atoms and subatomic particles that we cannot see with the naked eye. Therefore, relying merely on our sensory perception for our beliefs and faith is not correct.

Faith rests on belief based on cognitive understanding and

knowledge. Faith also rests on belief based on presumptions. Faith rests on experiences of life through generations of human beings. Blind faith, as they often call it, is also based on true, practical life experiences, which cannot be explained by applying the existing principles of science. Atheists call such blind faith superstition, because they simply discount and dismiss the existence of God. But blind faith, too, has a sound basis, whether it is rooted in real life experiences or simply in a sense of human insecurity.

A person who remembers God constantly is weaned from wrongdoing and leads a progressive life. A person who has led a morally upright life and performed his duties diligently tends to remember his master, God, during his dying moments. That is a sign of liberation of his soul. He gets emancipated from the multiple miseries of mundane existence and the ensnaring bondage of life and death. He is in sync with God—a phenomenon which has been metaphorically expressed as reaching the abode of God.

A person who naturally, and instinctively, remembers God during his last moments of life is one who is qualified for salvation through his sublime karmas. After death, his soul attains bliss. Shri Krishna was one such soul who had attained salvation much before his human incarnation. He possessed the divine attributes of a perfectly righteous human being. His actions as seen and studied through the epic Mahabharat show this. He knew exactly the right meaning of dharma and moksha. There was nobody better than him to guide Arjun in the battlefield. There was none who could illumine Arjun's way through the labyrinth of darkness that had engulfed his mind during those crucial moments of his life.

This verse brings out the message that if we remain conscious of the creator, God, continually on a day-to-day basis, we shall, no doubt, lead pious lives. Our actions will remain aligned with dharma and we shall carry our consciousness about the Creator to the last moments of our lives. Therefore, the modern human would do well to harbour a continuous feeling that God—his progenitor, preceptor, benefactor, friend, philosopher and guide—is always by his side. This feeling will give him a divine sense of security and a confidence that will accelerate his progress in life.

The last moments of a person are very crucial moments. It is widely believed that a few hours or minutes before death, the qualitative actions performed by a person over his life flash across his mind. He gets an overview of what good or bad deeds he performed in the course of his life. If the subconscious mind is flooded with memories of virtuous karmas performed by a person, the dying moments bring the thoughts of the Creator. That is an indication of emancipation of the person from the bondage of life and death.

Life is uncertain but death is a certainty. Therefore, death is probably a more important event than birth, simply because it is not only the gateway to a new life but its looming shadow keeps the living person in check and balance. Understanding and consciousness about the inevitability of death generates love for the limited moments of life which become dearer to the person. If you start valuing your time more, you begin to see the dire need to live for the day, hour, minute and moment. You start valuing life all the more. You relish every moment and utilize every moment. Life becomes more meaningful and satisfying. When you lead such a life, you will, for sure, carry this enjoyable existence beyond death. You will be in sync with God, who is the embodiment of bliss, and reach that blissful state yourself.

Chapter 42

The Aphorism of Salvation

Tasmaatsarveshu kaaleshu maamanusmar yudhya cha,
Mayyarpit mano buddhimame vaishyasya sanshayam.

Shri Krishna (on behalf of God): *One who surrenders himself to me through his mind and intellect and, constantly remembering me, fights all odds in his life, he will undoubtedly reach me and attain salvation.*

In these lines, Shri Krishna, the master of the Vedas and endowed with the wisdom of the perfect yogi, has revealed the mantra of moksha. He says that a person who constantly thinks of God and leans on Him, while at the same time does his worldly duties diligently, reaches His abode and is delivered from the bondage of life and death—the ultimate prize of living existence.

How does this happen? It is important for humans to understand the basic and fundamental facts that surround his existence and ultimate life objective. The mind of a human being is excitable and wavering. It makes the person hedonistic, undisciplined and immoral in the pursuit of his worldly goals. He goes astray in seeking the material objects of his desires. In the process, he forgets the tenets of dharma even if he knew them. He commits blunders. He breaches the laws of the land. He indulges in falsehood, deceit and treachery. And all this happens even while he knows the distinction between right and wrong, between propriety and impropriety, between the moral and immoral, between the righteous and unrighteous. This strange irony has been addressed by Shri Krishna.

If a man remains continually 'in touch' with his almighty Creator, his life becomes easier; his life's pathway becomes illuminated by the light of truth. He becomes receptive to divine guidance that is forever available to all sentient beings, including humans, the highest evolved species. Basically, it is the mind and the intellect which are the instruments of human action. If these prime instruments are well aligned with the Master who created them, then there will be no doubt that these instruments will work perfectly. There will be no doubt that they will help the human being get the best out of his life, in the shortest possible time.

The average man of modern times is very indifferent and apathetic towards labelled religion. You visit any modern bookstore and you will find books by the hundreds on the subjects of motivation, life philosophy, personal growth and success. But you will find few books on topics related to specific religions. In a way, it is a good sign which shows that the modern generation has grown more rational and secular. But the contents of these numerous books on self-improvement are lopsided, in that they do not consider the human being in his complete metaphysical setting. They extensively dwell upon the human mind—the conscious and the subconscious mind—but they seldom talk about the human intellect, even less about human soul and, often, completely ignore the entity called 'God'. They hardly touch the esoteric subject of salvation. Application of the known principles of physics and chemistry is not enough to explain the functioning of even the human body completely and comprehensively. Whatever we know about the human mind, based on study and research by psychologists, is also too meagre. Then how do we understand the human being fully well? We need the knowledge of human intellect and the concept of soul. To make a thorough comprehension of human behaviour, tendencies and aspirations, we also need the understanding of the eternal reality called God. It is in this context that the concept of salvation comes to the fore. The idea or concept of salvation lies embedded in the subconscious mind of every human being because the human being inherently seeks freedom and happiness. These can come only when an imperfect soul gets the helping hand of its perfect master, the creator God. Through surrender to the omnipotent and omniscient Master, the soul's task becomes easy.

When a human being stricken by pain, penury or privation feels helpless and depressed, he can, at once, improve his state of mind by surrendering himself to God. Despair will give way to hope and his intellect will begin to work in the normal manner. Once his intellectual faculty regains its composure, it will find the way to tide over the crisis by peacefully waiting for the tide of adversity to recede or even by working out a new, out-of-the-box solution to his problem.

Shakespeare had stated that 'brevity is the soul of wit.' True knowledge that gets you to your charted goal within minimal time is expressible in a few lines. The hymns of the Vedas exemplify this. But deep scholars of Vedic scriptures, like Shri Krishna, know the way to express the message of the hymns in simple and intelligible manner so that it becomes easy to grasp. That is visible in the epic Mahabharat, of which the Bhagwadgita is an episodic part. His two-line verses provide the gist of the entire philosophy of human living. The verses of the Bhagwadgita truly contain the essence of Vedic ideology that shows the way to human salvation.

Chapter 43

The Technique of Meditation

Sarvaddharani sayamya mano hridi nirudhya cha,
Mudhanaryadhayatmana pranamasthito yogadhaaranaam.

Shri Krishna: *Withdrawing the flow of all external senses—eyes, ears, etc.—inwards, a person should free his mind of all fleeting thoughts, fix his breaths at the topmost portion of his head and delve into yogic practice.*

In this verse, Shri Krishna explains and elaborates the technique of meditation upon God which helps a man to purify himself through spiritual alignment with his Master and achieve transcendental states. The creator God exists everywhere as a superior spiritual entity. But the human soul does not exist everywhere. It dwells only inside the body, in the centre of consciousness, called the heart. Only there, God can be experienced and realized. And the technique of alignment with God is provided by yoga.

Since God can be experienced only where the human soul resides, the place to experience Him is the heart where the mind, intellect and ego exist together. The mind, which is the epicentre of consciousness, is also the prime means for all human experiences. Hence, the mind needs to be freed of all stray thoughts, and through the power of the intellect, which holds control of the mind, the person has to meditate upon God.

Imagine through the mind that all breathing activity is centered at the top portion of the head. This technique helps in establishing connection with the higher spirit. The process is scientific because yogic practice is established on true scientific principles which consider the fundamentals of mind, body and soul, and the superior soul called God. The term yoga itself means accretion. When such an accretive connection with God is established, divine energy flows into the mind, intellect and ego of the yogi, which begins to purge the person of impure elements. It is these impurities that hamper human progress.

The Samveda is replete with hymns on the above subject. It talks of a divine nectar flowing from God to the human soul during the meditative state. This is the substance that actually purifies human mind, intellect and ego. It has the power of destroying the banal elements of passion, anger, greed, attachment and pride. It is the immortalizing nectar.

Modern science is less advanced than ancient science which was employed by our past generations who lived 5,000 years ago, and even by those who lived earlier than that. They understood the working of the human mind and the human soul. They, understandably, had space vehicles that could travel across distant worlds and galaxies. They had means of surface transportation that used simple natural substances, like water, mercury and flower petals, as fuels and were completely environment-friendly. We have to acknowledge these stark facts and also the fact that Shri Krishna was a super scientist, whose statements have unveiled the secrets of human existence.

This verse of Shri Krishna needs to be read in between the lines. It talks of the technique of meditation as a part of yogic practice. The actual complete yogic practice propounded by sage Patanjali consists of a series of eight steps. These are yama (non-violence, truthfulness, honesty, chastity and non-avarice), niyam (purity, contentment, perseverance, Vedic discourse and surrender to God), aasan (proper posture), pranayam (breath regulation), pratyahara (withdrawing thoughts from external objects and directing them inwards), dharana (mental focus), dhyaan (meditation) and samadhi (communion with the superior soul, God).

It is, therefore, seen that true and complete yoga constitutes the above mentioned eight-fold steps in sequence. You cannot go to the higher step without taking the lower one. If meditation appears as the seventh step, it has to be preceded by the six sequential steps indicated above. But what do we observe today? Meditation, mixed up with mental focus, is being sold out as capsule courses of ten or fifteen minutes. Yogic posture, exercises and breath regulation are separated from the eight-fold classical path and being marketed as brief sessions or regular practice courses, with additional coaching facilities. The whole thing has been overly commercialized. That is the reason why commercial yoga is not giving the desired benefits that can be derived from classical yogic practice.

Notwithstanding the above, meditation is today a recognized form of therapy for heart disease, depression and psychosomatic ailments in general. Its utility as a stress-alleviating means is widely known. We get the important message from this verse that systematic and complete yogic practice has enormous potentialities. It can uplift man comprehensively. It has nothing to do with any branded religion, sect or cult. It can make super humans out of ordinary humans.

We need to understand true yogic practice and follow the advice contained in this verse to develop ourselves physically, mentally, intellectually and then spiritually for self-actualization.

Chapter 44

The Knowledge of Deliverance

Idam tu tey guhyatamam pravakshyamyan suyatey,
Yanam vigyaansahitam yagyaatwa mokshayase ashubhaat.

Shri Krishna: *O saintly Arjun, now I will relate to you the ultimate principles of living, which are scientific in nature and content. Following these principles will deliver you from all miseries.*

Shri Krishna, as we know, was an enlightened soul who had reincarnated from the state of salvation. He came for the purpose of performing a specific worldly task—the task of resurrection of dharma in a human society that was witness to rapid decline of moral values and righteousness. He displayed all attributes of a perfect human being. He was an ace scholar of the Vedas, fully accomplished in the art of diplomacy and warfare and, above all, a complete yogi, who had vanquished the primal evils of passion, anger, greed, attachment and pride. He preached what he practised and practised what he preached.

Shri Krishna conveyed to Arjun, through the seventy verses contained in this book, the core metaphysical truths, the doctrine of karma and the broad principles that guide a human being all the way from mundane success to salvation. Ordinary human beings hardly understand the concept of salvation. They also do not understand the concept of the soul or even the subtle spiritual entity called God. The understanding of the purpose of human life and the interrelation of God, man and the physical nature is connected with these concepts. Therefore, ordinary human mortals tend to go perplexed and paranoid when confronted by challenging situations of earthly life. They often slip into states of confusion and dilemma.

The above is exactly what happened to Arjun. When he saw Bhishma, Dronacharya, Karna and his half-brothers pitched in battle against him, he was overcome by kinship feelings and lost the urge to fight. He thought, and quite erroneously so, that it was better to eke out an existence by begging than to live after slaying his own kinsmen. He forgot his prime duty as a warrior. He forgot his dharma, which enjoins upon a person not to hold attachment. Attachment clouds the intellect. Arjun's intellect had indeed become clouded. Shri Krishna cleared it. He was the man of the moment.

The Creator is super intelligent. He knows about His human creation much more than the human being knows about himself. God is omniscient. Man is of limited knowledge and understanding. Man doesn't know many things about his own self, let alone the outside world. He constantly struggles, rises, falters, falls, recovers, moves on, and through this process makes his way through the jungle of life. He is handicapped by his gross limitations of physical capacity, intellectual prowess and knowledge. Therefore, he needs the support of his creator God. He needs to be constantly in touch with Him. Shri Krishna explains the way to do it.

All knowledge has come from the Creator. No man can be credited for any single strand of knowledge. Archimedes discovered the principle of flotation. He did not create the principle. Newton discovered the law of gravitation. He did not create this law. Kepler discovered the law of planetary motion, and not created the law. All principles and laws were created by God. The entire universe is His creation. All His objects of creation work according to scientific principles. All the objects and systems created by Him work with perfect scientific precision. The precession of the equinoxes on the earth, the periodicity of appearance of comets, the regularity of natural events called solar and lunar eclipses, etc. are testimony to the above statement. The universe, including this earth, was created 1,960,853,118 years ago. All knowledge was handed down to the first humans, following the onset of creation, in the form of Vedas, from where the above figure comes.

When the universe is so old and mankind has been in existence for such a long period of time, it is only natural that mankind would have passed through multiple stages in its evolution. Knowledge is primal, and understanding, assimilation and application of this knowledge by humans has been going on for ages and eons. Humans, being innately of limited intellectual power, have lived with half knowledge, incomplete understanding and ill-conceived ideas through stages and ages. There are enlightened ones among humans who are endowed with high understanding and perfect knowledge of the Vedas. Shri Krishna was one such human being who guided the faltering humanity steeped in ignorance. The science of metaphysics and spirituality is something that needs to be explored, understood and followed by modern man. In this lies the solution to all problems besetting humanity today. In this lies the key to human deliverance.

Modern man, who is under passionate influence of science and scientific implements, needs to understand that the spectrum of science extends beyond the bandwidth of the present scientific theories. Science is yet to elucidate many phenomena of nature and unfold many a mystery of life. With this perspective will come a natural curiosity to learn about spiritual phenomena. That will pave the way for rapid resolution of today's pressing problems—climate change, economic disparity, poverty and deprivation, chronic disease, crime, terrorism, et al. Every problem has a scientific cause and a scientific cure. The knowledge of cause and cure is available to us and only needs to be systematically applied.

Chapter 45

Seeing God in Everything

Aham kraturaham yagya swadhaham hamaushadham,
Mantroaham hameyvajya mahamagniraham hutam,
Vedyam pavitronkaar rik saam yajureva cha.

Shri Krishna (on behalf of God): *I am yagya, the ritual of oblation; I am the offering substance of this oblation; I am the medicinal herb in this offering substance; I am the transcendental chanting mantra of this yagya; I am the ghee used in this yagya; I am the sacrificial fire and all other substances offered in the yagya. I am Omkar, one who is worthy of knowing, and I alone am the Vedas.*

In this verse, Shri Krishna conveys on behalf of the creator God that He is the essence of all things. He explains it through metaphorical expressions in the context of yagya, the sacrificial ritual prescribed in the Vedas.

God conveys through this verse that persons who see Him in all things as the prime working power become action-oriented like Him. The action referred to here is the action of yagya. He restores the sick to health through the power of medicinal herbs created by Him. Hence He is the offering substance in this vast participative activity called yagya, which purifies the air and provides health benefits to sentient beings. He is the revitalizing mantra of life. Persons who try to perceive God with this understanding begin to act like Him and become the revitalizing force in the society. Ghee, as the substance offered to fire in yagya, kindles the simmering fire of the yagya. In a similar way, God loves his subjects and kindles the fire of noble action in his human subjects. In an agnihotra yagya, the sacrificial fire is the leading force that spreads the purifying fumes in the atmosphere. Through this purification process, as mentioned above, all sentient beings are benefitted. In a similar way, God is the leading force in the entire universe. His actions continually benefit all living beings, who are His subjects. His actions are purifying and elevating. His actions promote our welfare all the way.

Everything that you see around—the sun, the moon, the stars, the sky, rivers, mountains, oceans, trees, shrubs, animals, insects, humans and the objects made by humans—symbolize God because they are His creations, directly or indirectly. The skyscrapers, swanky palaces, fleeting cars, cruising airplanes and the shop floor robots working in factories also symbolize God because they are the creation of man who was created by Him. Therefore, it is logical and appropriate that we see all things as the symbols of the almighty Creator.

Seeing God in everything is also a part of the yogic practice. Since yoga means communion with the supreme divinity for deriving transcendental benefits, seeing the Creator in all things helps in establishing connection with the Creator. This eternal message has been subtly given by Shri Krishna through metaphorical expressions in the context of an agnihotra yagya.

Modern world is witness to humans looking at everything from the transactional, commercial angle. In today's world, many persons, on performing some action, immediately start expecting the reward thereof. A student working hard expects that he will pass his examination with distinction. An employee working hard starts expecting increment, bonus and promotion. An industrialist investing in expansion of his manufacturing facilities will start expecting a surge in revenues.

A country offering economic aid to another country expects that the latter will open up its markets for the former's products.

If you go to the birthday party of your friend's child and give an expensive gift, you start expecting a return gift.

Modern man appears to be overly obsessed with the self. This needs to change for the betterment of his life, and this will change if man begins to visualize God as the essence of all things. Once he begins to do that, his focus will shift from the self to others, who, like him, are also the subjects of God.

When we do something for others' benefit, we automatically become eligible for rewards from the Master of the universe. This concept needs to be assimilated by humans for developing a work culture, which is going to be more fulfilling and, at the same time, more rewarding.

Doing something for others is yagya, and God subtly observes and operates every yagya that takes place in the world of humans. Imbibing the subtle message of this verse of the Bhagwadgita will make modern man more collaborative, cooperative, caring and selfless. These sublime qualities will develop based on the understanding that God's perfect system of justice will reward your efforts at the right time and in the right manner. Hence, man will also become more productive if he follows this philosophy.

Chapter 46

Offer Everything to Him

Yatkaroshi yadashnaasi yajjyhoshi dadaasi yat,
Yatpasyasi kaunteya tatkurushwa madarpanam.

Shri Krishna (on behalf of God): O son of Kunti, whatever work you do, whatever you eat, whatever substance you use as oblation, whatever you donate as charity, whatever penance you perform—offer all that to me.

Shri Krishna again tries to simplify the divine injunctions of the Vedas for daily practice in human lives. Normally, while doing any mundane task, a person harbours a worldly purpose behind the performance of that task. If he were to perform that task as an offering to God instead of performing for some earthly purpose, he will establish a mental and intellectual link with God. This will help him to avoid indulging in ignoble tasks, execute daily tasks more proficiently, perform noble tasks without becoming proud and, above all, develop a selfless attitude in life. This will help him to attain happiness, success, contentment and, ultimately, salvation.

A person who has the concept of an almighty Creator also knows His prime attributes. He knows that God is omnipotent, omniscient, compassionate and just. He knows that He is the ruler and regulator of the universe and delivers the fruits of actions to His human subjects. Therefore, by surrendering his actions to God, a person rids himself of worry and anxiety, because he is able to free himself from obsession with the results of his karmas. He becomes detached. By offering his actions to God, he is also able to overcome selfishness because, consciously or subconsciously, he continually feels that all his actions are for God and nothing in this material world belongs to him. He becomes virtuous and better oriented towards the welfare of his fellow beings because of his belief that his Master, who is just and all-powerful, is continually promoting the welfare of all living beings.

A man who offers all his worldly actions to the creator God also rids himself of pride. He becomes humble because he surrenders his perceived right to the fruits of his karmas to his divine Master. He begins to possess a continuous feeling that he is the child of God who, being just and compassionate, is continuously taking care of him. He feels that he is the servant of God and being a good servant means doing the best work for himself and others without having anxious expectations of rewards. The sense of servitude to God also brings humility in him.

In today's life, people seem to be more expectant, judgemental and demanding than before. We start expecting the fruits of our actions immediately after they are performed. Our anxiety begins the moment we complete our task. We need to imbibe the message of this verse in our daily life to be free of the burden of expectations and results of our karmas. We need not be burdened with the expectations. We need to burden our Creator with the strength and intensity of our karmas, so that He bestows upon us the desired results, maintaining perfect justice, which He always does. Offering our actions to God is a living philosophy which needs to be practised to appreciate its significance. If we offer our action to God, our action will become selfless and refined at the same time. This is the essence of karma-yoga that has enlightened the life path of multiple generations of humans.

Imagine a corporate honcho working in the competitive world of business. Engaged in the field of microcomputers, he is heading a transnational corporation as the CEO. His organization produces devices that find application in process automation and control. His organization has a well-defined corporate strategy as per which it is supposed to develop and produce devices for enhancing utility to industrial customers in terms of production cost reduction and increased economy of scale. His working methodology and approach need to have a sharp focus on customer utility, like in every business. To meet the requirements of market competition and rapidly obsolescing technology, he needs to innovate and work against uncertainties.

But if his working procedure is coloured by an approach to play safe, to protect his job—without taking the strategic calculated risks and to maintain his own status quo—his action is neither customer-oriented, nor in tune with his corporate strategy, nor in sync with the spiritual laws governing life. If his approach be such that he dedicates his actions to his Creator, he would work for utmost satisfaction of his customers and give his best to his role set, without bothering too much about his own job security. In that case, his actions will be most professional and productive. Best results and rewards will accrue to him for his efforts. That is the approach we should follow in our professional lives.

Many of us tend to be myopic in our roles set in life, looking closely at our selfish interests and working towards short-term gains for the self that are immediately visible. Obsessed by self-interest, we lose focus on our larger duties and responsibilities. Offering our work to the Creator will always prevent this. It will also prevent our deviation from the path of objectivity, honesty and truth. It will bring more happiness and peace in our lives, not necessarily greater wealth.

We are independent, conscious entities but we are dependent on God for knowledge and for the fruits of our actions that we perform independently. With the right understanding in our minds about our setting and relationship with God, we shall not swerve from the right course of action, action that is the harbinger of success, prosperity, happiness and progress.

Chapter 47

Understanding Him Further

Jyotishaam hamanshumaan nakshatranaamaham shashi.

Shri Krishna (on behalf of God): *Among the radiant luminous objects, I am the sun. Among the stars, I am the moon.*

Shri Krishna goes on to further elucidate the identity of God, pronouncing on His behalf. There are numerous effulgent, luminous objects in the vast universe. Among these objects, He is the sun, the prime source of life sustaining energy for the earthlings. This is also a metaphorical expression for the creator God. He is the prime source of all knowledge and knowledge is the light that dispels the darkness of ignorance. The sun's effulgence illuminates the earth and the sky visible from the earth. God's effulgence permeates the entire universe. God's effulgence manifests itself as the light of knowledge.

The one sun that we see from the earth is not the only sun in the universe. The universe has many celestial objects like the sun and many solar systems like ours. Definitely, there are many more celestial habitats of living beings like the earth in this vast universe. The Vedas talk of sun in contextual reference of human beings inhabiting the earth. Such reference extends to other living beings inhabiting the earth-like planets elsewhere in the universe. All such planets are illuminated by their respective suns. This fact has recently been corroborated through exploratory researches by modern astronomers.

Many luminous stars are visible in the sky. Of these, some are self-luminous, and others shine through reflected light emanating from these self-luminous celestial objects called suns. The non-luminous objects are planets and their moons. The earth has only one moon. Planets Jupiter and Saturn in our solar system have multiple moons. In the night sky, one observes numerous shining stars. The moon is the biggest and brightest shining object visible at night. The metaphorical expression of God as the nearest, brightest and most beautiful of the twinkling stars conveys Him as the entity who is an embodiment of truth and infinitely beneficent. Because of these attributes of the Creator, He holds a charm and appeal that is incomparable like the appealing beauty of the moon in the night sky.

God as a spiritual entity is the epitome of perfection. Anything which is perfect and complete symbolizes Him and reminds one of Him. These examples enable mankind to conceive the inconceivable and decipher the indecipherable. It becomes easy to comprehend Him if we approach the subject rationally and systematically. It becomes easy to grasp the ultimate reality if we proceed with faith built on reasoning. Reasoning gives human beings the perspective to understand things profoundly and completely.

Today's generation wants all the good things of life without necessarily believing in God or practising formal religion. A large section of this generation wrongly thinks that religion or God is a subject beyond the scope of science, or it is irrational and unscientific to be a theist. Science is the systematic study and analysis of anything. Science is the basis of the existence of man. Science forms the basis of the existence and operation of the entire universe. Modern man should understand this core truth. Therefore, he should be clear and convinced about the necessity and power of faith in the almighty Creator. He should further understand that behind his inherent quest for fulfilment lie principles and precepts that are eternal, and these were revealed by the same Creator. That is the perspective required to help the confused and perplexed generation of today.

To help build up faith in God through logical understanding, countless metaphors can be used. Metaphorical expression for God with reference to the sun and the moon also conveys that God is the superlative entity in terms of each and every positive attribute, be it expanse, closeness, beneficence or beauty. He is the greatest and the brightest. Through such expressions, it becomes easier to comprehend Him. That is what Shri Krishna, the master of yoga, has done; he has explained the infinite through comparisons drawn from the finite world of human mortals. Once man understands the concept of God, it becomes easier for him to relate with God because humans innately seek the fulfilment of desires. Human desires are fulfilled through benediction of God.

Conceptualization of God through allegorical examples from nature will make modern man more comfortable with himself and his surroundings, because he will constantly feel his own size, importance and existence inconsequential before the vast universe and its regulator, God. He will tend to surrender his ego before the Creator and believe that the Creator will solve all his problems—real or unreal. That nagging sense of insecurity will give way to positivity and hope. Hope will sustain him and steer him successfully through the jungle of life.

Chapter 48

His Greatness

Rudranaam shankarashchasmi vittesho yaksharakshasaam,
Maharshinaam bhriguraham, meru shikharinamaham.

Shri Krishna (on behalf of God): *Among the Rudras, I am Shankar; among the Yakshganas, I am Narad. Among the sages, I am Bhrigu; and among the mountains, I am the Meru Parvat.*

Rudras are the living entities who are the harbingers of death and destruction. Shankar was an ancient sage who, as a powerful yogi, is credited with the destruction of many evil and demoniac humans inhabiting the earth. Shankar is revered and remembered for his sublime actions and is regarded as the greatest Rudra in human history. But taking the matter beyond the realm of humans, God is the greatest destructive power in the universe. He destroys the evildoers through systematic and inexorable application of the law of retribution. God metaphorically refers to Himself as Shankar, the greatest among Rudras.

Yakshganas are the sentinels of human assets and human habitations. In Indian mythology, the term Yakshganas refers to the guardians of natural treasures hidden in the earth and under the roots of trees. The term also refers to the sentinels of human treasures and habitations. Narad, in Indian mythology, is described as the guardian and messenger of devatas, the noble human and celestial beings. He was a great compiler, interpreter and disseminator of information. Through this, he kept the devatas informed and alert about dangers. God is omniscient. Man often suffers because of lack of knowledge and guidance. He is unable to gauge impending dangers. God knows everything. If man remains aligned with his Creator and His laws at all times, he will be able to foresee dangers and can take advance remedial action.

Among the sages, God refers to Himself as Bhrigu. Bhrigu was an ancient sage who has been credited with compilation of much of the matter contained in *Manusmriti*, the famous scripture and guiding light of humanity through ages and generations. His knowledge about celestial phenomena and human institutions was unparalleled. The aphorisms given in *Manusmriti* about human life, those on the subjects of education, marriage, profession, governance and dharma, are fully relevant and meaningful even today. His contribution to *Manusmriti* has made it a great scripture, which is a source of invaluable guidance to human beings.

Among the mountains, the Lord refers to Himself as the Meru Parvat. In Hindu, Jain and Buddhist cosmology, Mount Meru is a sacred mountain with five peaks and is considered to be the centre of all the physical, metaphysical and spiritual universes. Its greatness and significance are unique, metaphorically comparable to those of God, the supreme Creator.

What is understood from the above is that God is unique, superlative, purest and greatest. His attributes indicate this in unmistakable terms. A conscious knowledge of these attributes carried in the mind will provide the modern man a heightened sense of security, because he will constantly have the assurance that the greatest power supports him at all times, everywhere.

Mankind has probably never been as insecure as it is today. In modern civil society, what we observe all around is fierce competition—in academics, sports, business, professions, politics. More often than not, devious strategies are formulated for beating the competition. Machiavellian modes are devised. This generates threat and fear. Ordinary persons' minds become homes to anxiety and worry. The meaning of this verse, when assimilated by a person, will surely and certainly provide a protection against fear and insecurity.

Besides reinforcing his sense of security, the message of this verse exhorts a person to strive for excellence in his duty. Any field of endeavour you may be in, you will like to achieve excellence in that field, drawing inspiration from this message. Because the examples of excellence are from the real world, not from the world of fantasy or imagination. Such excellence is achievable and within reach. Live examples, as role models, are there to motivate us. We have a role model for courage in Hercules, a role model for perseverance in Thomas Alva Edison, a role model for determination and that never-say-die approach in Abraham Lincoln.

It is in working towards excellence that human freedom and happiness lie.

A person striving for excellence means that he is trying to become more proficient, skilled, diligent and efficient in the discharge of his worldly duties. He is endeavouring to make a better utilization of his resources—his physical and mental strength, skill set, time and money. He is trying to bring more smiles on the faces of those served by him. He is trying to become a better human being. He has, before him, eminent personalities who have distinguished themselves in their respective fields through the use of sublime qualities, through high perseverance and performance. He is emulating them and refining himself all the way, while also creating a future of greater freedom and happiness for himself.

Chapter 49

Comprehending His Attributes

Ashwatthah sarvavrikshanaam devarshinaam cha Nara,
Uchhayi shrawasamshwanaam siddhanaam kapilo muni.

Shri Krishna (on behalf of God): *Among trees, I am the peepul tree; among the superior sages, I am Narad; among horses, I am the horse with high set ears. Among the enlightened ones, I am Kapil Muni.*

The peepul tree is a giant tree that lives for hundreds of years. It has a large canopy with wide, heart-shaped leaves. It is the only tree which emits life-giving oxygen during both day and night. Other plants and trees absorb oxygen from the atmosphere and emit carbon dioxide at night. The peepul tree is the sole exception to this. This superior characteristic gives the peepul tree a special place in Indian mythology and culture. Like the peepul tree which is the source of invigorating oxygen through day and night, the creator God is the perennial source of rejuvenating energy.

Among the sages, God refers to Himself as Narad. Narad had thorough knowledge of the six Angas—pronunciation, grammar, prosody, explanation of basic terms, description of religious rites and astronomy. All celestial beings revered him for his knowledge; he is supposed to be well-versed in all that occurred in ancient kalpas (time cycles) and is termed to be conversant with nyaya (logic) and the truth of moral science. He knew the science of morals and politics very thoroughly. He was skilled in drawing inference from evidence, and very proficient in distinguishing inferior things from superior ones. He was capable of arriving at definite conclusions about religion, wealth, pleasure and salvation. He was the master of the Sankhya and Yoga systems of philosophy, conversant with sciences of war and treaty, proficient in drawing accurate conclusions and judging on hazy issues. He was a thorough master of every branch of learning. A sage with such superlative qualities is metaphorically comparable to the omniscient God.

A horse with high set ears is the most superior breed among horses. It displays the best qualities and characteristics ascribed to horses. Such a horse is the perfect vehicle for travelling and battles. Being superior and superlative, it also attracts metaphorical comparison with God, who is man's best vehicle for all earthly activities.

Among the enlightened ones, Kapil Muni holds comparison with God. Kapil Muni was the founder of the famous Sankhya school of religious philosophy. This school occupies a unique place in religion as it stresses the importance of non-violence in human beings. Buddhism and Jainism are based on this prime philosophy. For his unique contribution to dharma, Kapil Muni is regarded as the greatest of seers and sages. That is why Kapil Muni is metaphorically compared with God.

When humans become refined and develop sublime qualities, their attributes can be compared with those of

God. That is why all these metaphorical expressions appear in the Bhagwadgita.

One of the causes of tensions in the modern world is the absence of a uniform and universalistic ideology. Among the seven billion human inhabitants of the globe, more than one billion are atheists. Millions are agnostics, sitting on the borderline of faith. They think that help of motivators, success coaches and mind management experts can enable them to solve all their problems, and so they try to go that way. But this does not happen successfully in practice. There is a yawning gap between theory and application. The life philosophy principles appear to be very catchy and attractive in theory but are equally difficult to implement in practice. The mind is very difficult to control and regulate. When human beings practise life management lessons, they invariably realize there are some missing links in their practical application. They may not be able to understand the missing links, though. And these missing links are actually the spiritual ones, related to soul and the super-soul, God.

These missing links will get closed when the concept of God as the embodiment of excellence is absorbed by humans. The gaps between theory and human application will begin to be filled with the understanding of God and His attributes.

As mentioned before, God almighty is beneficent like the peepul tree which has a wide, thick canopy and emits life-giving oxygen twenty-four hours of the day. It keeps on purifying the air for hundreds of years of its life. God continually showers His benediction on His earthly subjects. Understanding Him in this manner strengthens human faith in Him and also increases devotion to Him. Increase of human devotion to God means more commitment to the service of fellow beings and preservation of the purity of environment.

Hence, an understanding of the Creator is very basic to the resolution of all mundane problems and there is no better way to understand the Creator than to know His attributes and qualities. He has no image or idol or shape or form. He can be known only through His superlative qualities.

Chapter 50

The Best Among All

Airavatam gajendranaam naranaam cha naradhipam,
Aayudhanamaham vajram sarpanamasmi vaasuki.

Shri Krishna (on behalf of God): *Among elephants, I am Airavat. Among humans, I am the King. Among the weapons, I am Vajra and among the snakes, I am Vasuki.*

Airavat is a mythological white elephant who carries Lord Indra. It is also called Abhra-Matanga, meaning 'elephant of the clouds', and Naga-malla, meaning 'the fighting elephant'. Abhramu is the elephant wife of Airavat. Airavat has ten tusks and five trunks and is spotlessly white. It is also known as Erawan in Thai. It is referred to as the king of elephants in mythology. It shows all the perfect characteristics ascribed to the elephant.

Among humans, God is the monarch or the king. This expression carries clear logic since the king's attributes and role are comparable to those of God who rules the larger kingdom called universe. God is omnipotent. The king is also all-powerful in his mundane sphere.

Vajra is described in mythological texts as the ultimate weapon which never fails in a battle. It was used to destroy the asuras (ignobles) by the devatas (nobles) in ancient mythological tales. It is made from special materials bonded in such a unique way that the most powerful of explosions cannot break it. In metaphorical terms, it is the divine weapon of God, referred to as Indra. With this He slays the sinners and evil persons.

Vasuki is a nagaraja, one of the king serpents of Hindu and Buddhist mythologies. He is a king of the nagas and has a gem called Nagamani on his head. Manasa, another naga, is his sister. Vasuki is Shiva's snake. He is known in Chinese and Japanese mythologies as being one of the 'eight Great Dragon Kings'.

In all the above examples, superlatives are used for description. The best, biggest, brightest, strongest, tallest and toughest among things are the epitome of perfection and are comparable with the perfect God. This is a simpler and easier way to understand the creator God and His divine attributes. Direct comparison between the material and the divine is not possible. Hence, metaphorical comparison is used to describe the divine entity called God. Most of the human beings who possess grossly inadequate intellectual power can comprehend God through such allegorical or metaphorical examples.

God is beyond human sensory perception. He can be understood only through a comprehension of his unique qualities. In comparative terms, these qualities can be visualized in worldly or celestial beings and even objects. This is the way to understand the Master of the universe. In the modern world, we have laws and legal institutions like courts to dispense justice to persons who have been wronged by others. But these institutions often fail to provide proper justice to plaintiffs. We find district-level courts pronouncing judgements which fail to satisfy the litigant and are immediately contested in high courts. The high courts modify or reverse the judgements which are again challenged and the cases move on to the Supreme Court.

Such things are especially observed in the case of criminal suits involving important personalities belonging to the exclusive elite section of the society. A case in point is the corruption case against the former Chief Minister of Tamil Nadu, the late Jayalalithaa, who was convicted and sentenced to a jail term by a lower court in Bengaluru only to be later acquitted by the Karnataka High Court.

Justice not only gets delayed, but also derailed and denied. We must understand that human courts and judges will always be liable to deliver imperfect justice, because humans are innately imperfect of knowledge, intelligence and character.

It is only God who can and does invariably dispense perfect justice in each and every case. He completes the incomplete justice delivered by the human judges.

Sinners, moral delinquents, lawbreakers and the corrupt may hijack mundane justice but cannot escape the due punishment from the Creator, whose divine weapon, the Vajra, metaphorically represents His power of bringing the evil to perfect justice.

Modern-day humans would do well to gain an understanding of the creator God through examples suggested in this verse, so that the aura of enigma that has surrounded God is cleared and there remains no contradiction or conflict between science and religion. Such understanding will also resolve the differences between multiple religions and sects, thus sparing humanity of the fallout of continuing conflicts arising from differences in religions and ideologies.

Chapter 51

More Allegories

Varun yaadasamaham, yama sanyamtamaham,
Prahlad sarvadaytyanaam kaalah kalayatamaham.

Shri Krishna (on behalf of God): *Among the aquatic living beings, I am Varun; among the justice dispensing persons, I am Yama. Among all rakshasas, I am Prahlad. Among the testing forces in the world, I am time.*

Varun is the Hindu demigod of water and the celestial ocean, as well as of law of the underwater world. In the Hindu pantheon, the different attributes of one creator God are allegorically represented in different ways with multiple names given to Him.

Among those vested with the responsibility and role of dispensing justice, Yama is the entity who dispenses perfect justice to human beings for their earthly deeds. Yama is another name of God arising from His attribute of perfect justice deliverer.

Prahlada is a male name that means 'filled with joy' or 'excess in joy'. It is the name of a character in Hindu mythology. In literature, Prahlada was a 'daityaking', the son of Hiranyakashipu and the father of Virochana. Prahlada is the name of some of the eternal beings residing in the supreme realm known as Goloka as per the *Brahma Vaivarta* and other similar literary texts. He was known for his high virtuosity, devotion to God, humility and good behaviour. These great qualities make him stand out from all other members of the rakshas community through the corridor of history.

God has countless names and multiple attributes. He can be comprehended through His attributes and qualities. His attributes extending over His vast, infinite expanse need to be exemplified using mundane comparisons for ease of understanding. God is the embodiment of joy and so He is likened to Prahlada, the bundle of joy. This message further clarifies the concept and attributes of the Creator for His ordinary human subject. He is the epitome of bliss, so much so that remembering Him, praying to Him, engaging in service of His subjects and meditation upon Him are acts which bring joy to human beings.

Time is undoubtedly the greatest testing force in the universe. It puts everything to test. It puts everyone to test. It creates testing conditions for objects, persons, other living beings—both individually and collectively. It lays bare secrets that intrigue human beings for decades and centuries of existence. It is a great leveller and also a great teacher. It is the continuous witness to everyone inhabiting the universe and everything that goes on in the universe. Therefore, time, as an entity, is likened to the all-powerful God who is facilitating the refinement of sentient beings by subjecting them to trying and testing conditions.

Modern physicists have analyzed and elucidated time as an entity very well. The theory of relativity enunciated by Einstein brought out the interrelation among matter, energy and time. That time has been created through motion of celestial bodies was discovered by scientists long back. What is important for today's persons to realize is that an intelligent Creator is behind the celestial bodies under continuous precise motion. Time never stands still because the earth will never stop rotating on its own axis and revolving around the sun. This twin motion will continue till the dissolution of the universe. Time will witness everything and everybody. Hence, human efforts, human patience, human perseverance and all other human qualities are tested by time which creates different circumstances for such testing. This conveys the sublime message that man should always value time and make the best use of it by continuously refining his knowledge and character. It is also brought out by this verse that life will never stop throwing challenges at you. Life has never been and will never be a cakewalk for anyone. Life can never be a complete bed of roses for anybody. With this understanding, humans should lead their lives.

God is associated with bliss, and bliss is associated with God. In mental perception, the linkage of God with human bliss can act as a great comforting and destressing balm for the human being. Stress is the biggest problem that humans are grappling with today. Technology has made living easier but life more stressful. We need to burst the bulging balloon of stress that is tormenting our lives. We can do it by regulating our lives, utilizing our time in the optimum way. God's concept provided in this verse will help us to do that.

We note through the above discussion that God can be understood through multiple attributes belonging to Him, through multiple examples, comparisons and metaphorical expressions. Such expressions are for the larger sections of humans who find it difficult to understand the concept of God since He cannot be seen, heard or touched. He is not the subject of cognitive or physical senses. He is the subject of the real human self, called soul, and can be perceived only at the spiritual level. In the next verses appear some more such earthly comparisons with the divine.

Chapter 52

Identity Patterns

Mriganaam cha mrigedroaham vainateyashcha pakshinaam,
Aksharanaam kaaroasmi Rama shastrabhritaam aham,
Maasaanaam maargshirsho ahmritunaam kusumaakarah.

Shri Krishna (on behalf of God): *Among the wild animals, I am the lion. Among the birds, I am Garuda. Among the syllables, I am the first and fundamental syllable 'Aa'. Among the archers, I am Ram. Among the months, I am Margshirsh** *and among the seasons, I am Vasant.***

Here again, God's identity is being highlighted through more examples from the mundane sphere. The best and the biggest, the strongest and the smartest are comparable to Him. The most competent and capable and also the most caring and comforting entities are like Him.

The majestic lion, who is the swiftest and strongest among wild animals, represents Him. He rules the jungle like God rules the universe.

Garuda is a mythical eagle-like bird. It was the largest

---
*Corresponding to November
**Spring

and most powerful among birds. In modern times, its closest descendent is the eagle or kite. Garuda is the subject of numerous mythological tales. It used to feed on snakes. The eagle and kite too devour poisonous snakes.

God is represented by the fundamental syllable of the divine language, Sanskrit. From this syllable are derived all other syllables and hence, also, the entire fabric of the language. And from this divine language are derived all the different languages of the world as we know them today. The fundamental syllable referred to in this verse is, therefore, the etiological root of all media of communication.

The legend of Ram is too well known to merit separate discussion. He was the most skilled among warrior archers known through history. The arrow shot from his bow got the famous name, Rambaan, meaning an arrow that can never fail to strike its target. The term is used in folklore as a sure-shot remedy for any problem. The legend of Ram lives on even, supposedly, 1.3 million years after his death.

Among the months of the year, Margshirsh from the Hindu calendar corresponds to the month November from the Gregorian calendar. It is the most moderate and pleasant month of the year which does not show extremes of hot or cold or rainfall at any place on the earth. Arguably, it is the most comforting month in the year. The almighty God is the most comforting entity for all sentient beings. All troubled souls find relief in His divine lap.

Among the seasons, Vasant is the season of renewal and rejuvenation. It brings fresh green foliage to trees; it drives animals into the mating mode. It is the harbinger of everything that is fresh and fulsome in nature. It is moderate, bright and sunny. Indeed, it is the best and most enjoyable among the seasons. God is the embodiment of joy and mirth. The spring season represents Him as the harbinger of joy to sentient beings.

You can go on exemplifying the almighty Creator and the process can provide countless examples drawn from the worldly sphere. His identity patterns are infinite.

What do you gain by a knowledge of the Creator's identity patterns? God, in His infinite wisdom, knows that He cannot be comprehended by ordinary humans. That is precisely why He passed on all these examples and comparisons from the worldly sphere through Shri Krishna.

A piece of computer hardware (personal computer or PC) is assembled at the production shop floor of a PC manufacturer. Imagine that an ordinary person is using the PC as per usage tips given by his friend. Imagine further that this PC set has no brand label or any software link to the manufacturer. Hence, he has no knowledge of the manufacturer or its engineers involved in design, production, R&D and service functions related to the PC. Can he use the PC well? Can he get it serviced? Can he get improved versions of the PC?

A human being without knowledge of his Creator is in a similar predicament. He must understand his Creator and His attributes well to use his own body, mind and intellect in an optimal manner. If he knows the Creator well, he will be able to tap His infinite beneficent energy through means such as worship and yogic practice. He must know the Creator to rise and progress as a human being, the finest creation of the Almighty.

Proper knowledge about the Creator and His attributes is bound to reinforce human faith in Him. Today's civilization presents a picture of crisis of faith. And this crisis of faith in the higher power is the basis of many ills of the society, because a large set of problems emanates merely from human arrogance. Faith in God makes man humble. A humble person is better programmed for progress.

Chapter 53

Know Him Further

Vrishninaam vasudevo asmi pandavanaam dhananjaya,
Uninaam aptaham Vyas an kavinamushana kavi.

Shri Krishna (on behalf of God): *Among the persons of Vrishni lineage, I am Vasudev Krishna. Among the Pandavs, I am Arjun. Among the sages, I am Vyas. Among the poets, I am the poet Ushna.*

Vrishni lineage refers to the Yadav clan native to the central Indian plains. Shri Krishna belonged to this clan. We know Shri Krishna was a human being of superlative qualities. He was a great scholar, spiritualist, warrior, diplomat and above all, a great yogi. He was an outstanding personality in so many different ways. He was one of those super-refined persons who set trends for many future generations—trends in thought, behaviour and action.

Among the Pandavs, Arjun was the most balanced personality. He did not exhibit the human weaknesses shown by his brothers Yudhishthir, Bhim, Nakul and Sahdev. He was the most valorous and also most committed and focused in his tasks among all his brothers. He did not possess the intemperate nature of Bhim, or the tendency to indulge in gambling shown by Yudhishthir. He was candid about his weaknesses and was always in a corrective mode in that regard, seeking the guidance of Shri Krishna.

Among the sages, Vyas is credited with the compilation of the divine Vedas in the form of transcripts. He was the greatest scholar of the Vedas and his compilations are being used by the present-age humans, more than 5,000 years after his death. He was the greatest seer and narrator and wrote the epic Mahabharat.

Among the poets, Ushna was the most famous one in history. He was a legendary figure and is still remembered as the greatest among poets. His compositions arouse deep passion and stir the emotions of even the contemporary persons.

God has infinite names, corresponding to infinite qualities that He possesses. Every such name signifies a sublime and superlative trait. Persons, who say God is an enigma, fail to understand this fundamental fact. Everything that is purest, best or flawless represents Him. He is the epitome of perfection. He is very simple to understand and identify. Hundreds and thousands of things in this vast universe that exhibit perfection are shining examples of godliness. How can He be shrouded in mystery, as many ignorant persons say? He is the most obvious entity alongside us. Shri Krishna had done a marvellous job of driving home this stark truth.

What will the modern-day human gain through an understanding of the superlative attributes of the creator God? Understanding the Creator would make way for understanding the self because man is God's creation. Most of today's humans are at a loss to understand who they are, where they have come from and where they are to go. These most fundamental questions continue to confront and confound contemporary humans, as they confounded their ancestral generations. Understanding of the self will pave the way for real progress of the present generations, progress which is multidimensional and multifaceted, progress which will bring happiness and harmony to all places, not just in selected pockets of the globe.

Comprehension of the superlative attributes of the Creator will, naturally, reinforce faith and devotion in Him. Faith can move mountains. It is the most potent instrument of human development. Devotion to God with all those superlative attributes will make the devotee strive for perfection, in order to become like Him. This will drive every person for life-elevating karmas. This will make him successful in his endeavours and, above all, a better human being.

All positive human attributes, like kindness, compassion, selflessness and erudition exist in God. Therefore, a person tends to remember God when one sees a positive quality in another person. Remembering the Creator will keep him subconsciously connected with Him, which will be to big advantage of the concerned person. Superlative qualities in some persons bring adulation and make them worthy of emulation by others. And others do tend to emulate them, which helps in their own development, which, in turn, brings them nearer to the Creator. When we see in others such things as refinement of character, honing of skills or acquisition of knowledge and erudition, we, consciously or subconsciously, think of the Creator who facilitates the development of a human being.

It also follows from the message of this verse that God is a subject of passion as much as of reason. The Vedic scriptures describe Him comprehensively and clearly. Devotion to Him works through passion, just like the composition of poetic verses by persons driven by strong emotion.

Chapter 54

His Opulence

Naantoasti mama divyanaam vibhutinaam parantapa.

Shri Krishna (on behalf of God): *My opulence is infinitely huge; my divine attributes are countless.*

There is hardly any scriptural text in the world that provides such elaborate and exhaustive explanation of God as the Bhagwadgita does. It provides such a succinct and practical account of an abstract entity called God, that even a child can understand His concept through such account. It shows through numerous examples that the Creator manifests Himself in and around you in a million ways. His expanse is infinite, His qualities are countless but He is knowable. He can be understood, and understood well. He can be perceived and His divine energies can be tapped by His human subjects for their benefit and betterment.

His opulence is in His eternal ownership of the entire universe. He is the primary creator of the vast universe. His human subjects work upon the tiny bits of matter to meet the ends of their sustenance. He is the creator of the inert matter visible in the vast universe in its huge combinations of colours and contrasts. He is also the creator of the live entities roaming about their living abodes—the 8.4 million species of animals and plants, including human beings.

In most of the foregoing verses, just one thing is explained essentially—the concept of the Creator. There are countless ways to explain Him. There can be countless examples to elucidate Him and demystify Him, if some persons think that He is enveloped in a veil of mystery. The truth is that He is neither mysterious nor enigmatic. He is apparent and obvious, starkly visible to the inner eyes and is an existential entity.

One minute of contemplation in the balanced frame of mind reveals His great opulence to you. And at the same time, your entire lifetime may not be sufficient to describe His qualities and characteristics comprehensively.

Man is finite. His creator God is infinite. Can the finite explain the infinite? Yes, the explanation is possible but cannot be exhaustive. Man will run out of words, expressions, similes, metaphors and allegories but cannot explain Him fully. Man will run out of time but cannot put a full stop to this tale of explanation that describes the divine Creator.

His opulence is visible all around you in one look. It eloquently explains His existence, vastness, power and greatness.

Man's life is full of struggle and strife. It is challenging. It has always been like this through the course of history. The finite and imperfect man needs a support to meet the enormous challenges that life throws at him. If man understands that an infinitely powerful and resourceful entity, who is omnipresent and omniscient at the same time, is always with him to help and support him, he will be freed of worry and anxiety. He will also get over fear. His life will be filled with happiness and joy. That is what man wants, above everything else.

An understanding of the Creator's opulence, coupled with

faith in Him as his prime benefactor, will strengthen a person's belief that God can and will fulfil all his material desires. This is what an ordinary person wants. The ordinary person doesn't know the meaning of salvation nor does he consciously seek salvation. He wants to resolve his daily pressing problems or seeks the fulfilment of his desires. A jobless person desperately seeks a job. A childless couple seeks the joy of parenthood. A patient of chronic illness wants to be cured. An artist seeks recognition. A lonely person seeks a relationship. A pauper seeks wealth. A wealthy person seeks power and fame. An anxious person seeks security... The list is endless. All of these persons stand to gain from a conceptual comprehension of the Creator's opulence.

Much more than the above, a profound belief in the Creator's infinite opulence will convince every human subject that the material desires that he seeks to fulfil can be fulfilled because everything comes from the realm of the Creator. He only has to tap the power of the infinite. The means and modes of acquiring the objects of human desire will involve perseverance on the part of the human being himself. But this perseverance becomes a pleasant and enjoyable ordeal when backed by faith and conviction. This struggle and this hard work will become a motivator to the ordinary human being in the relentless pursuit of his goals. The belief in his benefactor's opulence will spur him into positive action and keep him consistently working towards his objective. This is the essence of all the theories and the various books of human motivation that are so popular and prevalent in contemporary times. This shows a simple and straightforward approach to the modern man for defeating the demon of depression. This belief really becomes the harbinger of hope to man. Positive hope is the strongest catalyst of human evolution.

Chapter 55

The Divine Revelation

*Pashyati mey parth rupani shatashoath sahasravasha,
anavidhani divyani nanavarnakritini cha.*

Shri Krishna (on behalf of God): *O Arjun, now you see my multihued, multifaceted form with a thousand faces.*

God is formless but to explain to Arjun the greatness and the unique characteristics of God, he reveals a giant, multifaceted form to Arjun, using his yogic power. He mesmerizes Arjun into seeing a huge, multifaced entity, so that he can better understand and appreciate the Creator.

God is not visible through the naked eye as He is a subtle, spiritual substance. It will not be possible to see Him even through the most powerful of microscopes because He is a non-material substance. Yes, it is possible to conceive Him and perceive Him through knowledge and understanding. He can be seen in His creation. Every object of His creation represents Him and gives an idea of His power and greatness. Because He is witness to everything, He is said to possess thousands of eyes and ears. His countless attributes mean He can be represented by countless faces, which indeed Shri Krishna revealed to Arjun through his mesmerizing power.

The multifaceted form that Arjun saw was not real. It was illusory since it was conjured and shown through the technique of hypnotism. But it was an excellent way to make him understand the divine Creator. Human beings understand better through daily life examples. When you teach children at the nursery or kindergarten level, you explain numbers to them through pictures, toys and models made of cardboard and clay. They understand all things through examples. That is why similes and metaphors work best in explaining things to humans at every age. Shri Krishna used this technique liberally in driving home the abstract concept of the real God.

When one has understood the concept of the Creator, one becomes better aligned with the immanent truths of life. One becomes more rational, focused and righteous, and, accordingly, achieves more of success and happiness, things that matter most to all human beings breathing on this earth.

Understanding the nature and attributes of the Creator is vital for tapping His infinite beneficent energy. Right understanding makes the way for right action and right action will get you all you desire in a systematic manner that will also facilitate your spiritual progress.

In today's times, it has become all the more important to demystify God. The glittering products of science and technology combined with the diverse sets of differing and diverging ideologies has bred a confused generation that doesn't take anything on face value and questions the validity of everything that does not carry glaring evidence. This verse does exactly that—it demystifies God for the purpose of building up the faith of all ordinary humans.

Whether God manifests Himself in physical form or shape has always been a subject of debate. Whether God can be represented by idols and images has been a subject of discussion and controversy for a long time in history. The truth gleaned from the Vedas is that God, being a spiritual entity, cannot be represented by any image or form and His worship also needs to take this fundamental fact into consideration. Today's generation has grown more rational, scientific-tempered and secular. It does not lay much importance on rituals found in orthodox religious practice. Hence, a random survey of today's youngster population could very well bring out the revelation that 30 per cent of the population surveyed is atheist or agnostic. That is where the problem actually lies. Atheists or agnostics are driven by logic but the sense of logic sustains them only as far as they are able to exercise it. Beyond it, the sense of logic doesn't work as it is constrained by the inherent intellectual deficiency of man. There comes the role of scriptures, of faith and of worship. There comes also the role of the divine message carried by this verse of the Bhagwadgita.

What this verse conveys in loud terms is that a person accomplished in yoga knows the art of hypnotizing. At the same time, the yogi is clear in his mind about the concept of nature, God and living souls as well as their interactive relationship. Therefore, to the modern man, it tells the power of yoga which strengthens the body, sharpens the intellect and enlightens the soul. What prevents the ordinary human from tapping the infinite pool of knowledge, power and bliss, i.e. God, is the absence of yoga. Yoga is the means and contrivance to unite with the infinite spirit and obtain transcendental benefits from Him.

The Bhagwadgita has been instrumental in kindling the faith of millions of human beings through the corridor of time and helping them to cross the turbulent ocean of human life. And today, this scripture can help in the resurrection of the dwindling faith resting on universal metaphysical principles. This verily is the need of the hour.

Chapter 56

Seeing the Invisible

Na tu maam shakshyasey drashtumanenaiva swachakshusha,
Divyam dadami tey chakshu pashya mey yogamaishwaram.

Shri Krishna (on behalf of God): Now, look up and see me. You will not be able to see me through these gross, external eyes. Therefore, I am providing you divine vision. Now see my opulence through the power of yoga.

Continuing his statements for and on behalf of the supreme power, God, Shri Krishna asked Arjun to see the giant form of God. Shri Krishna was trying to reveal the form of the formless God—a contradiction in itself. It was an illusory sight. It was created through hypnotic influence, using the power of yoga.

Where do the knowledge and technique of yoga originate from? Nowhere but the creator, God. All knowledge is sourced to Him. The power of Ashtang Yoga can be used to hypnotize a person into seeing things that the yogi wants him to see. Shri Krishna used this technique at the battlefield to convince Arjun about the power and opulence of God. It was important to do this since Arjun was overcome by negative sentiments and was losing the urge and enthusiasm to fight the war. It was necessary to enlighten him on the importance of accomplishing his duty. Duty and righteous karma carry with them the tags of reward. A person who neglects his duty does a grave injustice to others and his own self. Shri Krishna reminded Arjun about the regressive consequences of dereliction of human duty.

The importance of performing duty assiduously has been emphasized strongly in all scriptures and by all learned men. It is also true that knowledge of an existential entity in the form of the all-powerful Creator who regulates the entire universe, who is ever close to that person and watching all his actions, makes him more duty-conscious. The person, because of this awareness, is weaned from wrongdoing. He is able to overcome his doubts, dilemmas and confusions because of the faith in God, whose every action promotes the interest and welfare of His human subjects.

The revelation of the great qualities of the creator God through practical examples make a person better aligned with Him through reinforcement of faith in Him and, accordingly, makes the person more dutiful and morally upright. This reinforcement of faith has a catalyzing effect on human progress. It frees the person from stress, anxiety and fear. Freedom from fear means a lot. It makes him audacious and enterprising. It imparts a great, renewed zest to his life and makes him happier and more productive. Above all, it makes him a better human being.

This verse of the Bhagwadgita reveals the true meaning of yoga. In the modern world, yoga is largely understood simply as a regimen of physical exercises aimed at improving physical health. The role of yoga in improving mental health also is not known by many people. The verse brings out the fact that yoga's purpose is establishing connection and communion with God. Obviously, this communion cannot be done without a sound body and mind. Today, you find a plethora of yoga training centres all over. These centres can be especially seen in the Western world where yoga has gained tremendous popularity in recent decades. Partial understanding of yoga will give only partial benefits to its practitioner.

Complete understanding of the purpose of yoga is bound to deliver full benefits to its practitioner. If and when an average person, who is suffering from constipation, sciatica, arthritis, asthma or cancer, takes up yoga as a physical drill, he experiences health improvement in due course of time. But if he views yoga as a physical, mental, intellectual and spiritual training, he is likely to be more appreciative and enthusiastic about yogic regimen and will derive the best benefits from it. He will see yoga as a regimen of holistic development of the individual.

Swami Dayanand Saraswati, the religious and social reformer of nineteenth century India, was a bright exponent of yoga. He was an accomplished yogi. He was a complete personality. He displayed extraordinary physical strength and stamina. He was a picture of calmness, patience and perseverance. He showed, in full glow, all the human qualities of the head and the heart.

Today, we a have a living example of the power of yoga in Narendra Modi, the Prime Minister of India. A regular practitioner of yoga and meditation, he shows an outstanding physical stamina. He attends to a rigorous schedule of sixteen hours, without appearing tired or fatigued. He is an accomplished orator. The world knows him as a visionary leader and statesman.

There is much that yoga has to offer humans, and contemporary humans would do well to realize this fact. Yoga is not mysticism, it is science. Yoga is the means to see the invisible and fathom the unfathomable. It is the contrivance to connect you with the divine power existing within and without. It is the route to revelation of that divine entity.

Chapter 57

Description of the Divine

Anekavaktra nayanmaney kaadbhut darshanam,
Anekadivyabharanam divyaney kodyatayudham.

Shri Krishna: *The form of the Creator has multiple faces with multiple pairs of eyes. He is decorated with multiple attires. He wields multiple weapons.*

The creator, God, had been revealed through a conjured image by the power of hypnotism. The characteristics ascribed to Him were visible in this multihued and multifaceted form. Arjun could see human faces with eyes, ears and lips ad infinitum. He could see trunks with arms holding a variety of weapons. The attires of these human forms were sparkling with a divine brightness.

What was the purpose behind showing such a form? It was to help the finite comprehend the infinite. Human beings are spiritual entities with grossly limited power of comprehension. They are unable to understand the reality of things they cannot see with their eyes or hear with their ears or feel with the touch of their fingers. They can see finite objects. But the infinite is beyond imagination. It seems abstract. It becomes contentious, debatable and controversial in human discourse. This explains the huge number of religions existing in the world. Some are monotheistic, others polytheistic and some even atheistic. Seeing is believing, they say. Shri Krishna understood this very well. He was the instrument of this denouement of the divine. That is why the Bhagwadgita's verses are read and spoken even 5,100 years after they were first uttered. They seem to have become almost timeless, eternal.

Description of the divine gratifies the human soul. It reassures man that his all-powerful Creator is always by his side, watching him, helping him, guiding him and caring for him. He is the father, mother, friend, philosopher and guide, all combined into one. Grappling with his daily mundane issues and involved in his day-to-day chores, man tends to forget God. Revisiting this description reminds man of His overwhelming presence. It reminds him of His powerful existence and support. It also tells him loud and clear that he is a small fry, insignificant in this vast universe, regulated by the Lord. It conveys to him that his greatest friend is ever beside him and stands him in good stead always. He can bank upon Him and count on Him.

All he needs to do is to have unflinching faith and perform his karma doggedly and diligently.

Taking the meaning and interpretation of this verse at face value, any ordinary person will understand that God exists at all locations and is privy to all that is happening everywhere.

Imagine what would happen if present humans consciously and subconsciously kept in their minds the fact of God witnessing their every action! In today's civilized world, a corrupt bureaucratic functionary would suffer the pangs of conscience before demanding or accepting any illegal gratification as bribe. An infidel would feel uncomfortable within before embarking on his licentious affair. All criminals, thugs and moral delinquents would fear the retributive effects of their sinful actions before indulgence.

The mere thought and feeling of the Creator watching your every action will spur you into moderating and modulating every contemplated action of yours so that it does not attract negative sanctions from the society in the form of punishment. It will make you inclined every time towards actions which generate or maintain harmony and peace. The Creator wields infinite power of imposing retributive punishment for your vile actions. He is working in real time, 24/7 and 365 days of the year. He does not sleep nor ever takes rest even for a moment. Nothing can escape from His constant, watchful vigil. His description defies worldly parameters of description. If one were to describe His appearance, even if conjured, it would transcend the stereotypes associated with global regions or cultures. His attempted description would be so wide and inclusive that it would be universal in character. It would be acceptable to all, irrespective of religious affiliation or faith. It would be secular. Hence, embracing the philosophical undertones in this verse is bound to make the modern human secular, moderate, levelheaded and tolerant. The message has the potential to stem sectarian intolerance and hatred, widely witnessed even today.

What lies at the base of moral delinquency among humans? It is the lack of true knowledge, including the lack of knowledge and faith in the universal Creator whose retributive justice is immanent and eternal. Such knowledge and faith among humans can act as a powerful deterrent against crime. This deterrence will be built on the belief that divine retributive justice is always in operation as a broad-based dynamic system. It fills the gap in justice delivered by humans. It never fails to punish the guilty even if the human systems fail.

Chapter 58

The Tide of Destiny

Yatha nadeenaam bahavoambuvegah samudramevabhimukha dravanti,
Tatha tavami naralokvira, vishanti vaktranya bhivijwalanti.

Arjun: *Water in the rivers flows with vigour towards the oceans. In a similar way, O Lord, with the infinite expanse, these valorous humans are surging towards your multiple mouths which are seen to be swallowing them all.*

In the gigantic form of the Lord, Arjun saw various warriors from the battlefield of Kurukshetra gushing towards the mouths of the Lord. The Lord was seen to be swallowing them, which meant that they were being killed in the war. The picture conveyed that God had designed their death in the battle. Their death was a divine writ.

Water in the rivers flows gushingly to the oceans. In the same manner flow the currents of human destiny. No power can stop this flow because it is divinely ordained. What has been destined through the law of karmic retribution set in and operated by God is bound to happen. Nothing can check it. The scene displayed by Shri Krishna demonstrated the divine destiny of humans inhabiting the earth. At the battlefield of Kurukshetra, the warriors had come to meet their death, which had been designed even before the battle commenced.

The law of cause and effect is the basic principle behind creation, regulation and dissolution of the universe. There is always an intelligent cause behind every event. Behind the creation of the universe is the divine purpose of giving the eternal souls the means to evolve and attain perfection.

After the creation of the celestial bodies, the Lord creates sentient beings. Of the celestial bodies created in the universe, some, like the planet earth, serve as habitats of these sentient beings. The Lord provides the eternal living souls with bodies in the form of different species. They are given a means to evolve and refine and grow spiritually. This is the prime purpose of creation.

In accordance with the trail of their karmas, destiny of human beings takes effect as the trail of events and circumstances in their lives. The event of a person's death is also determined by the past karmas performed by him. God is the power which determines the time and mode of this last event of the person's life. This was demonstrated by Shri Krishna through his power of yoga as Arjun was hypnotized into visualizing a many-headed, imposing animate entity devouring the many warriors who were destined to die in the battle of Mahabharat.

It was a live description of the entire drama of human life and death.

This verse conveys eloquently that the entire universe operates according to an immanent law of cause and effect. This is a dynamic law, which means that it is operative continuously and at all locations. The entire edifice of Buddhism is built around the concept of the dynamic law of cause and effect. The law delivers perfect justice to humans across the globe in qualitative and quantitative terms. This law can also be termed as the law of divine retribution. When the concept of this law becomes deeply embedded in the human psyche, it makes the human being consciously accountable for his own actions.

In view of the above, modern man needs to revisit the principle of divine retribution and lead his life with a firm commitment to this principle. This is the principle which operates the vast universe. This is the principle which elevates humans. This is the principle which bestows on humans the fruits of their perseverant action. This is verily the principle which causes the creation as well as dissolution of the universe. It is working eternally. It is inviolable. It is synonymous with God.

There is still lot of confusion persisting in the human society about God and religion and destiny. This confusion tends to turn persons into disbelievers. The law of divine retribution, if clearly comprehended, will convince people about the universal operation of this prime principle. It will remove the veil of mystery enveloping many objects and phenomena in the world. It will demystify God and make many things crystal clear to the ordinary human beings. It will deal a death blow to superstition. It will enable mankind to see spirituality in religion and religion in spirituality.

Renewed conviction in and commitment to the principle of cause and effect will make modern man more humanistic. It will make him a more responsible member of his family, community and the global society. It will clear the lingering cloud of confusion in his mind as to whether destiny is greater or human karma. It will make the human being more focused about his role as a global citizen and more eager to contribute his mite to the betterment of the world.

Chapter 59

The Divine Writ

Yatha pradiptam jwalanam patang, vishanti nashaya samriddhavega,
Tathaiva nashaya vishanti lokaast vapi vaktrani samriddhavega.
Arjun: *Flying insects, like moths and mosquitoes, are attracted towards fire, and dash towards it to be destroyed. In the same manner, these human warriors are gushing towards your huge mouth to meet their destruction.*

Arjun describes to Shri Krishna the scene that he beholds. Using the right similes, he gives an apt description of what he visualizes. Death doesn't isolate a person from his divine Creator. He remains in his Creator's lap. The Lord who created him is also his destroyer. He is the death-dealing demon as much as He is the caressing Creator.

God is the be-all and end-all of existence. Everything in the visible physical world begins from Him and everything terminates at Him, too. He is the fulcrum of the entire universe. Your physical body, consisting of elemental matter belongs to Him because He is the master of the entire material universe.

He creates this body and He destroys it, too, at the appropriate time. You, as the soul, is beyond destruction or dissolution. You gain knowledge and experience through corporeal existence in a lifetime, and this accretion of experiential knowledge goes on through a series of lives. The entire philosophy of human existence is expressed loud and clear by having a look at the power of the supreme divine entity called God, and His role in the universe.

There are many actions that we all perform in our lives which are qualitatively intended to bring some desired, tangible results. But in the course of time, we find that the expected results did not come and events that occurred were far beyond our imagination. This, again, underlines the stark fact of human ignorance and human half knowledge. And this, at the same time, underscores the omniscience of the master of the universe, God. He fixes the reward of human efforts in a hundred per cent just manner.

The death event of a living being is completely controlled and timed by the almighty Creator. For a human being, the equation of his past earthly karmas and their inevitable effects has to be completed before it is time to depart. In the Creator's domain, this calculation is performed impeccably for every human being. Hence, death is always a new beginning for the immortal soul—a new period of opportunities for mundane karmas.

Death is a divine writ. The knowledgeable among men know it too well and live their lives accordingly. But those who think otherwise, come to shock and grief in the course of time.

In death lies dignity and deliverance when it occurs in a noble pursuit or as a part of our duty. Death is not the end of life. It is a milestone event in the eternal journey of the soul. The writ of destiny is made by the actions performed by a person. The scene presented in front of Arjun demonstrated this existential reality of human life. This underlines the importance of good karmas in human life—karmas that promote peace, harmony and welfare of all living beings.

In today's times, we know a lot about many things, but still not about human death. What happens to the human soul, if it exists, on death? Where does it go? Why is it that the dead persons never come back alive? Death remains the enigma that it was. This verse provides a concept of death which says that it is the creator God who takes away human life. The Creator is just. Whatever He does is for the good of His subjects. So death is not an event to be feared. This perspective will inject a fresh enthusiasm into life. The fact that life continues after death will make even the depressed, defeated and dejected develop a fresh zest for life, because the process of human karma and its reward will go on—even after death. There will be many rewards of your actions that may come after your death—in the new life thereafter. With this perspective, life will generate new hope for the hopeless and make the broken and crestfallen glow with expectation again. Life actually gives many opportunities. There is always that proverbial silver lining to every dark cloud, and depressing and dreary days are always numbered.

Let the modern man in the grinding mill of life understand that all in not lost in failure or defeat. This is exactly the message brought out by this verse of the Bhagwadgita. Let the defeatist thoughts also not torment us anymore. Life, being eternal, has a lot of promises in store for us and many more opportunities undreamt and unimagined by us. We only have to keep moving forward with a steadfast approach and things will fall in place inexorably. This phenomenon is in accordance with the law of universe, designed and operated by the omniscient and omnipotent Master.

Chapter 60

The Lord's Cosmic Form

Aakhyahi mey ko bhavanugrarupo, lokaansamahartumiha pravrittah,
Name namasteyastu sahasrakritwah namah purastadath prishthatastey.

Arjun: *I am struck by your gigantic form, by your blinding effulgence. Please reveal your identity; I understand that you are present here to wipe out these warriors. I bow before you, pay my obeisance to you a thousand times in every direction!*

Unable to believe that he had seen the almighty God, Arjun expressed his amazement and bewilderment at the sight. He had been totally hypnotized. The giant form that he was shown was simply out of this world and beyond human imagination. In today's world, we can explain it to be something like a scene from a modern science fiction movie with three-dimensional effects.

The form had blazing brilliance. It was a masterly pictorial representation of the supreme Godhead that humans so often discuss in their religious discourse. It was such a wonderful sight that it captured the complete attention of the beholder, who was totally immersed in it. It was entirely enthralling and completely captivating. It was a brilliant image of the unimaginable.

Wonderstruck by the fantastic power of his charioteer, Shri Krishna, Arjun sought to know his real identity. Looking at the vast Godhead figure in front of him, he overwhelmingly expressed his obeisance to it.

For most humans, God is an abstract entity, because He is not seen or perceived by the human senses. That is why He seems to be outside the realm of reality. Human belief in God rests on faith. Such faith may come from culture, tradition or indoctrination. It may also come from self-understanding and realization, as is the case with intellectually refined persons. Many great scientists of the past and present generations have been firm believers in a universal power called God. Faith in God naturally develops with human experience. The tumultuous journey of human life presents many ups and downs, many events which either generate this faith among atheists or convince the agnostics about the existence of the divine.

Arjun was a cultured Aryan of his times. He was a believer. But considering the manner in which he had been struck with dilemma caused by attachment, he needed a quick and firm correction of thought with a reassurance of the existence of the divine design of destiny that would spur him to positive, affirmative action in the great battle. Shri Krishna reinforced his fledgling sense of duty. He created the great scene to clear the cloud of confusion which had perplexed him at the crucial moment.

We see in the world episodes of train and road accidents, airliner crashes, earthquakes, tsunamis, cyclones, floods, volcanic eruptions and also epidemics and wars which take a toll on millions of lives. Since we do not see the creator God through our physical eyes, most of us tend to believe that all those deaths of humans were accidental or chance happenings. Nothing could be farther from the truth.

Just like a man's birth, his death is also timed by his Creator. That is precisely the reason why we humans need to live as the supplicants of the Master of the universe. We need not be in awe of Him as He is our prime well-wisher and benefactor. He provides us protection from catastrophes. We only have to understand Him and his eternal relationship with us. That will generate steadfast faith which will help us steer clear of problems and meet the various challenges that life brings.

In the light of the philosophical undertones of this verse, the modern man needs to revisit the concept of death. If man understands the phenomenon of death, he will understand better the eternal phenomenon of life. Life and death are two faces of the same coin. The bottom line is the fact that the soul exists eternally. The value of life and the necessity of good karmas shall be very well appreciated if the meaning of death is understood. By gaining this understanding, humans will begin to see death as the event of return to the abode of the Creator after the interregnum of life. Thus, life's value will be better realized. Today's humans are, as always, vying for a better quality of life, for deriving more value out of life—more happiness, more satisfaction. Valuing life will make humans value time, and valuing time will certainly make them more positive and productive. That will accelerate their comprehensive progress.

To get more out of life, a person needs to reaffirm his faith in the Creator, so that he can continuously engage in productive and welfare-oriented activity without developing any anxiety about the results of his karmas. He would require an unflinching belief in the power that is with him and supporting him all the way to deliver the just rewards of all his actions at the right time.

Chapter 61

Exposition of His Greatness

Naaham vaiderna tapasa na daanen na chejyaya,
Shakya aivam vidho drashtum drishtavaanasi maam yatha.

Shri Krishna: *O Arjun, the spectacular form that you have seen is such a form that can be seen neither through discourse of the Vedas, nor through penance, nor through charity, nor through performance of yagya.*

Again, this is an account of visualizing the invisible. God is invisible to the naked eye because He is too subtle a substance for them. But Shri Krishna presented a visible form of the formless and the subtlest. It was conjured. It was illusory. It was meant to reaffirm Arjun's faith in God in the critical moments. Dwindling of this faith is common in humans. Man's worldly life experiences are such that this faith in the Almighty gets shaken time and again. Many times, he gets so involved in the rigmarole of daily life that he virtually forgets God, His influence and His power. He loses faith in God. This is natural and is universally true. It was not peculiar to Arjun.

The power that runs the universe is unseen. The power that guides human destiny is invisible. The entity that maintains company with us eternally is beyond sensual perception. But He is the greatest power, unique, unparalleled, incomparable.

The Vedas are the primordial books of knowledge, the scriptures that were revealed by God. Study of the Vedas provides an insight into the characteristics of the Creator. Penance is a human action that disciplines the mind and brings us closer to Him through understanding, thought and mental perception. Charity gives us inner satisfaction and sublime happiness because we serve the subjects of God through it. And yagya is the ultimate mode of worship, the benefits of which have already been explained at length. All these activities enhance our awareness of God. They increase our understanding and appreciation of God. They cannot reveal God pictorially because God is not finite and so cannot have a shape or form or picture. Before Arjun, His form was dazzling and amazing and brilliant. It was a heavenly sight for Arjun. If anybody else would have seen it, he would have felt the same.

Revelation of the conjured form of the formless through yogic powers to Arjun was important in those crucial moments before the commencement of the greatest battle of that era. And, as we know, this revelation, coupled with the explanatory verses uttered by Shri Krishna had a salutary effect on the befuddled and paralyzed Arjun. He was back in tune with reality, coming out of the illusion, and ready and eager to perform his solemn duty as the prime warrior in the historic battle.

This verse of the Bhagwadgita brings out the nature of the entity called God. He is a non-material, non-physical entity. Hence, He cannot be perceived through the physical senses. There are no scriptural texts that show the means to see Him. No amount of penance or yagya or any virtuous karma can enable man to see Him through his external, gross eyes. It is important for the human being of the present times to understand this.

To conceptualize God, it is necessary for man to understand that He is not a physical entity. He is a spiritual entity. Once man understands this subtle concept, he will become better aligned with nature because he will realize God's infinite overwhelming presence and power. His thoughts and actions will tend to fall in harmony with the forces of nature. He will neither like to ravage natural resources nor will he degrade the physical environment, because he will see God as the spiritual element permeating everything, controlling everything and regulating everything. He will develop greater compassion for all sentient beings.

A majority of human beings in the present world may still believe in God but presumably do not carry the concept of God delineated in the Vedas. Let man be clear on the nature and concept of God as an infinite and all-pervasive spiritual entity. The very settlement of this concept in his mind will enable the average human being to live with less fear and more peace. If that happens, we shall definitely see lower incidence of crime and corruption in the civil society. We shall witness less violence and more peace all around. After all, the outer world is a reflection of man's inner world. If the inner world, i.e. our mind, is harmonious and peaceful, the outer world will be alike. The right perspective on life will give the right attitude to man. And attitude is what matters most. The right attitude will enable easy resolution of all problems besetting man. Life will become brighter and more beautiful.

Chapter 62

Unattached Karma for Salvation

Matkarmkrit matparamo madbhaktah sangavarjita,
Nirvairah sarvabhuteshu yah sa maameti paandav.

Shri Krishna (on behalf of God): *One who performs his actions for me, casting off all his attachments and passionate desires, becomes my devotee. He becomes even-minded and level-headed. He ceases to have passionate affection or deep hatred towards all sentient beings. Such person alone attains union with me.*

This is the criterion for becoming the favourite of the Lord. Shri Krishna has explained this criterion in most terse terms. The performance of human actions without any desire for reward means the actions are done as offerings to God, with the deep faith in His retributive justice. This faith forms the foundation of fast-track progress of the human being.

In the above process, man needs to cast off all his attachments with the mundane world. His attachments include his material desires, passionate wants, deep affections or strong feelings of hatred towards other beings. His deep-rooted desires for wealth, status, power, fame and material assets that accompany these will present obstructions in his spiritual growth. When these desires are gradually overcome, man develops mental equanimity and becomes intellectually balanced. He then views everything with a rational and realistic perspective and, above all, with a holistic perspective. His thinking, action and approach take into consideration his true purpose of living and true goals as a human being. Thus, he becomes spiritually refined, transcending the planes of a gross mundane existence.

A person who works his way up the spiritual ladder through transcendental means gets closer to God, and then, ultimately, attains union with Him. This union is not a physical union, as both the human soul and God are spiritual entities. It is a tuning of the finite soul with the infinite universal soul. It is a union without loss of individual identities. It is a sublime togetherness of the finite soul with the infinite God, with the former attaining supreme bliss.

Union with God is an extremely esoteric expression. It is beyond imagination and virtually beyond explanation. It is something that can be experienced through the technique of yoga. The Bhagwadgita is a set of sermons that revolve around yoga. Yoga is the instrument of human transcendence to the ultimate level of existence. This is the level defined by complete freedom and bliss. This is the level characterized by perfection of mind, body and intellect. It is marked by no human tendency for unrighteous thought, behaviour or action.

A majority of human problems and pains stem from selfishness. Contemporary humans need to imbibe this lesson and try to be more selfless. If the basic approach in every human action becomes altruistic, that action will make the performer's life tension-free.

Consider a working professional, say a police official working in a big metropolitan city. His set of duties includes tracking and apprehension of criminals in his designated area.

His approach should be to work towards keeping his area free of crime, and not to be a party to the present practice of collecting corrupt money. A small retail fruit seller at a street corner of a city should do his work with the approach of satisfying his daily customers by providing best quality fruits and displaying courtesy. His primary aim should be customer satisfaction with reasonable profit, and not just profit maximization. A lawyer should work with an approach that enables his client to get justice in the minimum possible time, and not with an approach that maximizes his fees through long, protracted court proceedings. Inclination to maximize benefits to others through human karmas is the watchword here. This is the big lesson that one draws from this verse of the Bhagwadgita.

The above suggestive statements constitute a special perspective on professional interactions. Making businesses customer-oriented and customer-caring does not mean that these businesses should run at a loss. A healthy balance between profit and customer benefit needs to be established. Transparency and honesty should form the watchwords in business operations. A selfish, inward-looking approach doesn't bring big rewards to a professional or his customer. That professional should work with an approach that will create a win-win situation for both. This approach is the selfless approach; this approach is that of a devata—someone who consciously wants to give, not to take.

Contemporary humans, therefore, need to develop a different perspective on life—that of enhancing the benefits to others and giving them maximum happiness. In the larger spiritual context, this becomes a philosophy in which one is focused on serving and satisfying others. Service to humanity is service to the Creator. Being service-oriented is the true way forward for material as well as spiritual growth; being materialistic and self-oriented is not.

Chapter 63

Scientific Explanation of God

Yatha sarvagatam saukshamya daakaasham nopalipyatey,
Sarvatra vasthito dehey tathaatma nopalipyatey.

Shri Krishna: *The entity, God, exists in all places, including every nerve and every vein of the human body but, being ultra-subtle, does not gel with the body parts, just like the ether, which exists all around but does not mix up with other material objects.*

Shri Krishna has gone a step further in explaining the seemingly abstract entity called God. He offers a scientific explanation. He compares Him with ether which is present all around us but maintains its separate identity. God, as a superior spiritual substance, is present all over the material universe but exists as separate and distinct from it. This is the scientific concept of God gleaned from the Vedas.

A superior subtle spiritual substance that is God is also separate from the souls of sentient beings dispersed all over the universe on its multiple celestial abodes—the planets. The souls, the inanimate matter and the superior spirit called God remain distinct from each other. This scientific fact has been succinctly explained by Shri Krishna. Matter is dead or inanimate, created from the cardinal constituent elements—earth, water, fire, air and ether. The laws of physics, chemistry, mathematics, thermodynamics, statics, magnetism or electricity apply to matter. But these laws are not applicable to spirit. The spiritual kingdom has its own different laws. We need to understand them. Only then shall we acquire a holistic understanding of a human being and of his creator God. Only then shall we be able to charter our way successfully through this dark, dreary jungle of the world with its many uncertainties and imponderables.

Science is the systematic study of anything. We need not confine systematic study to dead matter. We need to extend it into the spiritual sphere. We must understand the laws of the spiritual world populated by the countless living souls and one superior soul called God. Even the laws of the physical world of the dead matter have to be correctly and comprehensively understood by us. This is possible by assiduously following the text of the divine scriptures, the Vedas, which contain the principles and precepts of the entire material world. Our current knowledge of the material world is incomplete. It is half knowledge. It cannot solve all human problems and satisfy all human needs. This is evident from the afflictions to the present world which, despite tremendous scientific advancements, is unable to find solutions to the problems emanating from climate change and unable to find cures of intractable ailments like cancer.

When modern-day humans begin to understand God in scientific terms on the bedrock of logic, there is no doubt that non-believers will turn into believers through conviction, and not on the basis of blind faith. Faith itself will change in character—blind faith resting on superstition will be transformed into resolute faith founded on logical understanding.

Science and scientific advancements of the past few centuries have remarkably coloured human thinking and ideologies. Most people of the contemporary world regard present scientific knowledge as the ultimate knowledge and attempt to test the veracity of everything by applying the known principles of physics, chemistry and allied physical sciences. As per the message conveyed by this verse, God is omnipresent and can be understood through logical approach. Logical approach is scientific approach. The message will broaden the mental horizon of today's persons who will realize that modern science is incomplete. It is yet to reach the stage of development where it can lay bare the mysteries of the spiritual world. With this thought, people will explore the unexplored through knowledge enshrined in the eternal scriptures called Vedas. Scientific pursuit and application will acquire a new dimension—the spiritual one.

Grasping the underlying meaning of this verse, the concept of God will sink in the mind of the modern man. Once that happens, man will view the creator and controller God permeating the entire ethereal space. He will conceptualize God as a subtle spiritual entity beyond the purview of his physical senses. He will be able to connect and identify himself with God. This will always help him to live with hope. That hope will have a solid, steely foundation built with faith, and faith is enormously powerful. God is perceived through the medium of mind and intellect, and a scientific understanding of the nature of God makes such a perception possible. God is the greatest scientist and His messages contained in the Vedas are eternal precepts of scientific knowledge.

We need to develop a purer and more comprehensive scientific outlook. Divine sciences, if applied correctly, can pull us out of every conceivable trouble and every imaginable sorrow. They can help us achieve all our material goals and attain moksha, the ultimate stage in happiness and fulfilment.

Chapter 64

Illuminator of its Zone

Yatha prakashatyeka kritsanam lokamimam ravi,
Kshetram kshetri tatha kritsanam prakashayati bharat.

Shri Krishna: *The sun illuminates the various planets and their moons. In a similar way, the soul is illuminating the entire body.*

The subtle philosophical message underlying this verse needs to be understood. The sun is the source of light for all terrestrial beings. It illuminates all planets in the solar system. Even the celestial bodies called moons, revolving around their planets, shine through the incident light of the sun. This arrangement extends to all other solar systems in the universe. The sun emits energy, including visible light. In a similar way, the soul resident in the human body energizes the body. It is the source of consciousness. The sun has its own zone to illuminate. Similarly, the body is the zone of the soul.

When a person realizes that he is the soul and the body is his dwelling abode, he becomes aware of the primacy of the soul and of the fact that the body is inanimate and impermanent. He clearly comprehends the permanence of the soul. He becomes conscious of the prime reality that death occurs to the body, not to the soul.

Fear of death should not deter a person from performance of his sublime duty.

The soul is the source of physical energy required to keep the body alive and running. The soul itself seeks happiness and fulfilment, nothing else. But for this, it must overcome its ignorance and its propensity to swerve from the righteous course. Right knowledge and right action are needed for this. True scriptures—the Vedas and their explanatory texts, and above all, the scholarly interpretations by erudite persons—provide the right knowledge as nourishment for the soul. Thereafter, the soul has to make its own way forward through sheer willpower, using the body, mind and intellect appropriately. Mental discipline, then, forms the watchword of its progressive journey.

When the soul realizes its power, role and objective, it becomes focused and firm in the pursuit of that objective. This self-realization catalyzes it into progressive action. This verse of the Bhagwadgita comes back to the subject of soul after the discourse of divinity. This underlines the fact that man is his own liberator. Everything else—scriptures, scholars and the almighty God—are facilitators of this process.

How will the above knowledge help the modern man to lead a better life? Understanding of the soul is essential to understanding of the self and others. This understanding forms the foundation of right action—action that is progressive and that promotes peace in the world. A person who realizes that he is a spiritual entity who lives eternally, will at once become a realist. He will cease to live in a dream world and become more pragmatic. He will improve his relationship with his spouse, children, peers and other members of his community. He will begin to appreciate the abstract needs of the soul. Yes, he will begin to understand that the soul seeks bliss. Everything else that is desired in the world is incidental and secondary to this prime need of the soul. He will become a better human being.

Understanding that living beings are all creatures with souls will bring more compassion in the human society, and mindless killing of animals for food will reduce. Humans are designed by nature as vegetarians. Slaughter of animals in huge numbers for food on a daily basis is a big contributor to environmental degradation because of the disturbance of natural ecological processes that it causes. The largest environmental concerns associated with slaughterhouses are wastewater and water contamination. The United States of America alone has thirty-two slaughterhouses responsible for dumping fifty-five million pounds of pollutants into the waterways annually. The wastewater from slaughterhouses, as one can imagine, contains all sorts of obnoxious materials, known as suspended solids, including fat, grease and manure. Slaughterhouses are also responsible for large outputs of greenhouse gases, such as methane and carbon dioxide, both major contributors to climate change. These gases are created both in the process of slaughter and by further degradation of wastewater. As indicated above, wastewater contains a number of organic materials, all of which release methane and carbon dioxide when they decompose. Given the fact that fifty-five million pounds of pollutants are dumped into waterways each year in the USA alone, the amount of these gases emitted globally is enormous and is a matter of serious concern.

The clear answer and solution to the grave global problem described above is that modern humans turn to vegetarianism.

The clear understanding that soul is the master of the body can bring about revolutionary changes in modern medical practice. It can refine our methods of treatment and align them with mother nature and with Ayurveda, which is the last word in medicine.

The firm understanding and belief that human essence is spiritual and we all are specks of spiritual substance seeking salvation will be the greatest ideological revolution that can occur in the global society. It has the potential to transform each human being into a more useful and peaceful inhabitant of this planet. It has the potential to transform the character of global institutions for the better.

Chapter 65

The Scientific Basis of Human Karma

Satwam sukhey sanjayati rajah karmani bharat,
Gyanama vritya tu tama pramadey sajayatyut.

Shri Krishna: *There are three types of attributes residing in the human being—satogun, rajogun and tamogun. Satogun provides contentment and happiness. Rajogun drives a person into action, while tamogun makes him lazy. Tamogun veils his knowledge and distorts his understanding.*

This verse of the Bhagwadgita describes in very precise words the qualitative basis of human action. The attributes—satogun, rajogun and tamogun—are found in elemental matter which builds up the human physical body and is also the constituent of human mind and intellect. Hence, it is obvious that human action, which takes place through a working of the human body, mind and intellect, will be qualitatively shaped by these attributes.

To understand the broad spectrum of actions—moral and immoral, righteous and unrighteous—in scientific terms requires the knowledge of the above attributes. Man innately possesses a logical approach in his quest for knowledge. He has a natural tendency to behave rationally, based on his understanding of the right and beneficial course of action, even if that understanding is incorrect.

Human karma is satoguni if it promotes peace, happiness, harmony and progress in the human community. It is rajoguni if it produces ambition, action and arrogance in the human being. It is tamoguni if it causes indolence, stupidity and criminality in a person.

Human karma is satoguni if it is performed in accordance with truth. It is satoguni if it is done with a selfless outlook. Karma becomes rajoguni when it is done for selfish material gains, for self-aggrandizement. Karma is tamoguni when the motive is criminal and immoral.

The human being is a traveller to the destination of salvation. To reach any destination in the physical world from a certain location, one needs the correct route. Similarly, to reach the destination of salvation, man needs right knowledge, which comes from satogun. Then, what is further required to reach the physical goalpost is a travelling action. One may walk barefooted or ride a vehicle. This motive action which is the basis of various mundane activities comes from rajogun. The pathway is long and the journey rough. The traveller would need intermittent rest during the course of the journey. Yes, rest in worldly work routines is important, because it recharges the human being in his arduous journey. Tamogun provides this much-needed rest. Therefore, all the three material attributes play their part in human life. One has to use them when required, in a balanced manner.

The judicious use of satogun, rajogun and tamogun will enable humans to truly unfold the mysteries of life. Application of the knowledge of these gunas will make it possible to modify human mental traits and personality patterns in a scientific manner. If a person is lazy, it means he is having an excess of tamogun. One of the ways to reduce tamogun is by avoiding the intake of food substances which increase phlegm in the body. The other way is to perform aerobic exercises. A habitual delinquent has less of satogun. If we increase his level of satogun by a spartan lifestyle, including intake of pure and wholesome organic vegetarian food, and moral education and meditative practice, his criminal tendencies can be overcome. There are a thousand and more ways in which the judicious combination of the three primordial gunas of nature can make it possible for us to refine human mind and intellect, something which can be a potent tool to effectively tackle the problems besetting the contemporary world.

An average person, through his daily life, can understand the variation of the three gunas in his body, mind and intellect, if he applies the fundamental knowledge of these gunas to his own self. He can understand why he is intemperate and happy on different occasions. Based on the correlation of gunas with his lifestyle, he can keep himself in a fine state, physically and mentally. He can sharpen his intellectual faculty too. He can reap the best benefits out of his time and other resources.

Through scientific and systematic application of the three attributes of nature, we can, therefore, improve our functional efficiency in all fields of endeavour, utilizing time and talent optimally. Talent is both innate and acquired. By modulating the gunas and obtaining the right mix of gunas in various activities, we can achieve remarkable efficiency gains. Efficiency gains will naturally translate into increase of productivity, and this will generate more employment and produce greater wealth, globally.

No doubt, judicious application of the science of gunas will bring out far-reaching changes in our living patterns, in our systems—all for enhancing human peace and happiness. After all, that is what every human desires in the ultimate analysis.

Chapter 66

The Effects of the Three Attributes

Urdhwa gachhanti satwastha madhye tishthanti raajasah,
Jaghanya gunavrittistha adho gachhanti taamasaa.

Shri Krishna: *Persons with a preponderance of satogun rise spiritually, those with rajogun dominating remain in the middle state while persons with a preponderance of tamogun fall.*

The secret of true human progress, i.e. spiritual transcendence, could not be explained in a more succinct manner. The master key to reach salvation, the ultimate abode, is satogun. This explains why all the wealth of the world cannot guarantee human happiness. This also tells us that power and fame, too, cannot bring lasting happiness to the human being. Happiness comes from satogun, which brings honesty, moderation, compassion, detachment and humility in all human actions. When such virtues colour human action, the latter begins to uplift a person. It becomes transcendental. It becomes sublime and takes the person to the higher levels of consciousness.

But, as stated in the foregoing chapter, matter inherently contains all the three attributes. It is the balanced state of these attributes which is healthy for a human being and results in his ascent in spiritual terms. Spiritual ascent is true progress, for, man is essentially the soul. The soul needs no food or water. These are required by the physical body. The soul needs no wealth, because it is not a material entity. Yes, the soul seeks happiness. It seeks freedom. It seeks bliss. There are means on the material plane to get what the soul needs and desires. The body is the vehicle for the soul. The mind, senses, ego and intellect are the contrivances available to the soul to achieve sublime happiness. The soul has to use these means intelligently, prudently, effectively.

Rajogun triggers action. Well-directed perseverant action produces wealth. Wealth brings comforts and conveniences, but not happiness. Wealth provides limited satisfaction. It is gratifying in character. It gratifies a person by appeasing his senses, mind and ego. It cannot bring happiness to the soul because it is not what the soul needs.

Tamogun paralyzes human reasoning power. It pushes man into the zone of ignorance or half knowledge, which inevitably brings his downfall. It makes him indolent. Inaction and lethargy cannot generate wealth and push the person into penury. The end results are sorrow and suffering.

Satogun is better than rajogun, and rajogun is better than tamogun in so far as spiritual utility is concerned. But rajogun and tamogun have their own innate utilities, if maintained in moderation. The best mix for a person is a high proportion of satogun, with modest level of rajogun and low proportion of tamogun.

Modern science knows very little of the mind and mental phenomena, like memory, perception, intuition, premonition and clairvoyance. Through the understanding of gunas, it will be well-nigh possible to acquire a clear comprehension of all these. Mind is by far the most complex entity in the human or animal being. Mind is the pivot of a human being and is at the core of his personality. Through a knowledge of the attributes called gunas, it is possible to explain all human behavior, even predict it to a certain extent. It is possible to condition humans favourably and beneficially for all. Through regulation of gunas, you can regulate your own mental traits and perform all positive and successful action effortlessly. You can then achieve anything and everything in life. You can dream and fulfil all your dreams.

Knowledge of the three gunas and application of the same in human life can help to solve complex problems of the human society, like criminality and communal or religious intolerance. It can help to stem corruption from civilized society. Today's world is privy to a dangerous phenomenon called terrorism. We can surely work out a solution even to the problem of terrorism through application of the knowledge of gunas.

If a person is lazy and procrastinator, he has a predominance of tamogun in him. He has a predominance of tamogun also if he is confused, deluded, irritable and anxious. If a person is arrogant, overly ambitious and restless, he has an excess of rajogun. Thus, knowledge of the gunas can be a most effective armamentarium to counteract the baneful effects of tamogun and rajogun, which manifest in the form of prime negative mental states, such as anger and egotism.

The knowledge and application of the science of gunas, as indicated, holds the golden key to successful resolution of a wide variety of human problems. Taking guidance from the subtle message of this verse, we need to explore the mysteries of the human mind through the scientific principles of the three gunas. We will have much to learn and much more to gain.

Chapter 67

Transcending the Range of Gunas

*Samdukh-sukhah swastha samaloshthashma kaanchana,
Tulyapriyapriyo dhirastulya nindatma sanstuti.*

Shri Krishna: A person who transcends the range of the gunas will be called 'gunatit'. A person who views happiness and sorrow alike; who displays mental equanimity in favourable and adverse situations of life; who has developed the habit of internal traversal of the mind; who sees gold, silver, rubble or stone alike; who considers friends and foes alike; who has a wealth of patience and who considers his censure and praise alike—such a person is a gunatit.

What is it to rise above the three attributes of matter? It simply means changing the orientation of the self from the materialistic to the spiritualistic. The soul is not material by nature. It, therefore, cannot have either satogun or rajogun or tamogun. It can have knowledge, attitude, perspective or orientation. Such orientation can be materialistic or it can be sublime spiritualistic. If the soul gets entangled in the labyrinth of the three attributes, it becomes subject to the banal forces of passion, greed, anger, pride and attachment. It inevitably gets suffering and sorrow, though it never wants to suffer.

Mental equipoise in a person means the healthy attitude which will keep away sorrow. A person who develops the habit of looking inwards for solutions to his life problems gets the right answers because he communicates with the omniscient God. He directs the flow of his sensory energy inwards. That enables him to establish the link with the Almighty, who has all the answers to his questions and the solution to his every problem. Accordingly, he gets the better of fear, doubt, suspicion and worry.

Treating gold and stone alike means looking at both with the perspective of their creator, God. That is the healthy perspective which disentangles a person from the ensnaring grip of passion and desire. This sublime message was given by Lord Buddha some 2,500 years ago in human history, and this message has helped millions of humans to overcome sorrow and attain eternal bliss.

Treating praise and deprecation alike means remaining unaffected by both. It means not getting elated by praise and not feeling downcast in censure. It means maintaining an even keel. A person who is even-minded will not harbour hatred even for those who are inimical to him and he will also not have passionate love for those who are friendly to him. He keeps a balanced state of the mind.

Salvation lies in transcendence of the range of gunas, the three material attributes of nature. This is the core and crux of spirituality.

In the modern world, how many of us view happiness and sorrow alike? In success, most of us tend to exult and in failure, most of us sink into gloominess. How many of us view gold and stone alike? The powerful message of this verse provides us the key to the hidden treasures of life. We are constantly seeking these treasures, indulging in a mad pursuit of them, engaged in a rat race for acquiring them, but our means are not designed to actually reach them.

To achieve success and happiness, we need to put as much focus on our inner state of the mind as the existing focus on the coveted objects of our desire. We must understand the fact that our mind and heart are the real abodes of all treasures. The road to success will necessarily need a traversal through our conscious and subconscious mind, which will make us realize our weaknesses and strengths and pull us out of delusion. This great message emanates from this verse of the Bhagwadgita. As long as our entire focus remains on the external objects of desire, we shall remain continuously engaged in their pursuit with attendant impatience, restlessness, irritableness, frustration and grief. The internal traversal through the mind is intended to wipe out these negative emotions which are as much a roadblock in our material accomplishments as in our spiritual development.

Applying the divine message of this verse in modern life will convince us that the road to material success can be traversed through spiritual discipline where the daily grind of conscientious duty is what matters more than anything else. For getting what we desire, we do not necessarily have to run after godmen and motivators and life skills coaches. We are our own masters and our own guides. We need to rise above the dualities of material life and we shall begin to see the real beauty of human existence unfolding before us. We shall start getting the answers to the vexing questions that had been troubling and tormenting us in the past. Life will no longer remain a riddle. God will no longer remain a mystery. Everything will become crystal clear. Life will acquire a fresh colour of freedom and joy, not experienced before.

Chapter 68

Definition of the Saint

Maanaapamaanayo stulya stulyo mitraripakshayo,
Sarwarambh parityagi gunatita sa uchyatey.

Shri Krishna: *A person who responds to his honour and dishonour alike and possesses a level-headed approach towards both friends and enemies, and above all, has renounced worldly chores—such a person is a saint and worthy of reverence.*

Shri Krishna has indicated in this verse the qualities and characteristics of a saint. A saint is a person who has transcended material desire. He possesses desires but his desires are all spiritual, like that of his master, God. A person with spiritual desires will have inclinations which are all virtuous. He will not show even a trace of evil because all his tendencies and actions will be towards promoting peace, purity, progress and prosperity in the world.

This is the real regimen of spiritual ascent. This is the practical path of progress for the human being. This verse of the Bhagwadgita tells it all, and tells it precisely and clearly. It defines a saint and also defines a moral derelict. It conveys to us what it takes to reach the higher goals of life. It presents a pragmatic picture of a pious person. It provides a practical perspective to the most esoteric subject of spiritual development. In other words, it brings out clearly the characteristics of ordinary persons and of spiritually refined folks.

A person who has realized the core truths of life and his ultimate goal begins to lose passionate interest in worldly matters, rises above his involvement in the rigmarole of mundane living and develops a spiritual outlook on life. At that stage, he has renounced all mundane matters. He attains sainthood.

A saint is a good human being. Conversely, any good human being is a saint. A person doesn't become a saint by donning the tag of a religious sect or by performing the set of rituals specific to a religious school. A saint is one who is virtuous in action and spiritual in mental perspective. He finds worldly tasks and all mundane matters as the means to a higher end. He is more in tune with the realities of existence than the ordinary person. Because of such a dispassionate and detached outlook, he renounces his worldly tasks and focuses his attention on the divine.

Saints are worthy of reverence. They radiate an aura of warmth and compassion. Respectful interaction with a saintly person generates positive vibes and has a calming effect on one's mind. But the journey of an average human being from the ordinary to the extraordinary, to sainthood, is a tough one.

The adoption of the sublime message of this verse in modern-life situations is bound to render a new meaning to the word 'saint'. It will give a fresh new perspective to life in today's generation, which is living more in confusion than in clarity with regard to the basic issues of life. Far from being a symbolic entity, a saint will be understood as one who has risen above selfishness and material cravings and will be a role model, worthy of emulation by others. He can be one's friendly neighbour or the good Samaritan colleague at the workplace. In today's world, we have been witness to many tagged sectarian saints who have not risen above mediocrity and many who were even implicated in criminal acts. There are sectarian saints who are smitten by intolerance. That is why the members of the modern generation, especially the younger ones, are losing interest in orthodox religious activities. The world is apparently looking for a new philosophy, a new perspective on life where the goal and the pathway are both clear. When people start looking at successful human life as a saga of noble karmas, their orientation will start shifting from materialistic to the spiritualistic. Human life will discover new colours and shades of happiness, contentment, serenity and succour.

Today's world community appears to be involved in an economic rat race. After the rapid rise in the income and living standards of people over the last hundred years, thanks to modern science and technology, many developed and prosperous countries are witnessing a stunted or negative economic growth. Employment opportunities are shrinking mainly due to stagnation of technological growth, coupled with mass-scale computerization and automation. The developing world is grappling with its own inherited problems, including crime, corruption and poverty. Under such circumstances, a saintly outlook on life will balance things out considerably, through moderation of desire and curb on greed. A generous perspective, in which happiness of others is more important than benefits to the self, will resolve a large number of problems on the planet, including that of global warming, caused by huge and widespread emission of pollutant gases.

Chapter 69

Pathway to the Ultimate Abode

Maam cha yoavyabhicharena bhaktiyogein sewatey,
Sa gunaansamati tyayitaan brahmabhuyaya kalpatey.

Shri Krishna: *A person, who through unflinching devotion meditates upon God and serves His subjects, transcends the three attributes of matter, and reaches his ultimate abode of salvation.*

Meditation upon God maintains connection with Him, and serving His human and non-human living subjects puts a person on the fast track to the goal of human salvation. This is the essence of good human living; this is verily the gist of all human actions that are progressive. The verse emphasizes on meditation as well as service. Both complement and supplement each other.

The benefits of meditation upon the supreme spiritual power have been delineated in the foregoing chapters. It will be appropriate to reiterate here the core metaphysical truth that the entire material universe is filled with this supreme spiritual substance with infinite expanse. When the soul concentrates upon the super soul, divine nectar flows to the soul's appurtenances, which are the mind and the intellect. It purges these vital elements of their impurities. The impurities in mind and intellect are caused by a high proportion of rajogun and tamogun, which generate vanity, greed, passion and anger. This is the science of spirituality, and this fact needs to be understood by the academically trained persons of the current times to fully appreciate it and apply it to their lives.

A person, who while performing the yoga of communion with God also performs noble and virtuous acts that bring tangible benefits to others, thus promoting goodwill, harmony and love in the human community, and carries out actions that promote purity and wholesomeness of the environment, gradually unshackles himself from the bondage with the material world and establishes a tuning with God. The state of complete tuning with God is the state of salvation.

The route to the ultimate abode is slippery. There arise several situations when the human being gives in to the banal forces that afflict the mind and entangles himself in the vicious consequences of his indiscreet actions, often momentarily or briefly. He has to correct his course of action and realign himself with dharma and continue the journey.

Service of fellow beings without expectation of reward is a true, unattached service which brings the performer closer to God. This is altruistic service, which gives a person the true experience of the divinity dwelling within. It gradually and inevitably brings him in sync with this supreme divinity and into the condition of lasting bliss.

Service is the step on the ladder to liberation. Modern man needs to draw the message of service from this verse. Selfless service of other humans or animals and plants in the ecosphere generates a natural surge of happiness which can be better experienced than described in words. Mother

Teresa is widely remembered for her tireless service towards persons afflicted by HIV/AIDS, leprosy and tuberculosis and for rendering charitable service to orphans and the poorest of the poor. The Missionaries of Charity, an organization established by her, consists of about 450 brothers and 5,000 sisters worldwide, operating 600 missions, schools and shelters in 120 countries. The experience of these brothers and sisters is a living testimony to the power of service in delivering transcendental benefits to humans. In selfless service of other beings, a person forgets his own problems and afflictions, and assuages the pain of others. This increases his proximity to the Creator.

True service is that which is rendered without expectation of reward. If reward comes, it should be humbly accepted. Such service to man is service to God.

Warren Buffet, Bill Gates, Michael Jackson and Azim Premji are famous for outstanding success in their respective professional streams, but they are better known for the huge philanthropic activities they have performed.

It is quite easy to see that in modern communities, sects or institutions, which have service as their motto, the members are peaceful, dignified and prosperous. The universe bestows happiness on those who are committed to service in thought and deed. Service is the way of purification of the human self. This gospel has been lived by many and demonstrated time and again.

Philanthropists continue to live long after they die. Service is the basic element in philanthropy. It bestows immortality. Sustained selfless service provides bliss to humans while they live. After death, it leads them to salvation.

The state of bliss is reached when desire has given way to detachment, when proclivity for virtue has completely ousted weakness for vice. Service without selfish material motives puts a person on the fast-forward evolutionary mode. The whole matter of human evolution is a most scientific, logical and practical affair, evidenced by experience. Such experience is the stage and step in the ascent of the soul towards the highest goal.

Chapter 70

The Final Sermon

Sarvadharmaan parityajya maamekam sharanam vraja,
Aham twa sarvapaapebhyo mokshashishyaami ma shuchah.

Shri Krishna (on behalf of God): *Relinquishing all shades of worldly religions and duties, just come in my protective lap. I will free you of all sins. Grieve not, worry not.*

Man's natural quest for peace and happiness has always ensured that religions, sects and cults exist in the society. We have been witness to mainstream religions founded by saintly men or their followers. We have also been privy to the shades and variants of these religions. These variants, major or minor, run into hundreds and thousands in numbers. Not just the historical times, even the present world is witness to nearly three thousand religions and their variants. Every such religion prescribes a set of rules for their followers. The basic philosophies preached by these religions have major similarities and also major or minor differences. Some folks get confused by these differences. They lose belief in God and become atheists. Some of them remain on the borderline of belief and are termed agnostics.

Shri Krishna knew fully well the above unseemly situation.

He understood that ordinary persons would tend to have fragile faith, because of the innate limitations of human intellect and knowledge. At the crucial moment on the battlefield of Kurukshetra, it was very necessary to strengthen Arjun's faith and, accordingly, his commitment to duty. Such crucial and challenging moments occur from time to time in human life. The verses of the Bhagwadgita were uttered by Shri Krishna only for the purpose of providing guidance to humanity for effectively meeting such challenges.

Shri Krishna also understood well that human beings are always troubled by an inherent sense of insecurity, because life is uncertain and future is not known. Man has to live on moment-to-moment basis and move forward. Time flies and it is in the optimal utilization of time that human deliverance lies. Hence, a person needs to be aware of his divine creator and preceptor, and lean on Him like a child leans on his parents.

This verse of the Bhagwadgita tells man that he needs constant support and security of the higher beneficent power to help him navigate smoothly through life, with all its problems and uncertainties. God is that beneficent power who always extends a helping hand. But the prime requisite for tapping that power is faith—faith in His eternal existence, in His love for His subjects, in His infinite power, overriding authority and flawless justice. When a person has developed such a profound faith in the Almighty, he gets over worry, fear, sorrow and grief. God also guarantees that a person who has risen above the trivialities of mundane life and has established communion with Him, based on unwavering faith, gets all boons from Him, and is even delivered from the fallouts of his sins.

And why not? The Creator is omnipotent, omnipresent, omniscient and also compassionate. He is the embodiment of bliss. He wants His subjects to be in bliss, too. He is, naturally, facilitating human progress every moment so that His dear subjects attain bliss.

There cannot be a more universalistic message for the modern human being than the message conveyed by this verse. Modern man, by and large, lives in a crisis of faith. There are believers, half-believers and self-proclaimed rationalists who decry the existence of God. Many of the global citizens today are disillusioned with traditional religion. This is borne out by the constantly thinning attendance at churches in Europe and America, as also elsewhere. The younger generation is particularly cynical about religious dogmas and rituals. It questions the scientific validity of these rituals and sneers at the practices followed by the proponents of various mainstream religions.

The message of this verse of the Bhagwadgita has the potential of rekindling faith in a generation growing increasingly cynical and apathetic towards religion. It provides to the modern man the infallible concept of one-to-one interactive relationship between man and his Creator. Such concept transcends the variations of race, age, ethnicity, language, religious affiliation, nationality or geographical location of the modern global citizen. The concept of God, who is both personal and universal, can bind human beings as never before. At the same time, the resurgence and reinforcement of human faith in the Creator will serve to assuage stress and tension, which are so much in evidence today. It will relieve humans of the burden of expectations that generates such stress, which is taking a heavy toll on human peace and happiness across the globe. Faith is a very potent instrument of human emancipation. Such a faith will pave the way for the betterment of individual and collective life alike. It will generate the kingdom of heaven right here on earth.

Epilogue

The world today may be vastly different from what it was 100 or 200 or 1,000 years ago, but human beings are not much different from their forefathers. Those belonging to the previous generations had the same problems, pleasures and predilections which today's humans possess. Times have changed, technologies have changed, lifestyles have undergone transformation, but human weaknesses and strengths have hardly changed. Human nature, temperament and desires will not change. That is because of the immanent character of the human body, mind and intellect. The only thing that has changed on the planet is the grade and level of human knowledge, which humanity applies and continues to create newer systems of living and habitation. These systems evolve with time—for the better or the worse. The intention of humanity, though, is always to develop better systems that will serve it more efficiently. What ultimately comes out of human endeavour is a strange, kaleidoscopic admixture of good and bad, useful and useless, harmful and benign.

Core knowledge is eternal and immanent. It does not change. What changes is human understanding and application of the knowledge that is understood. Scriptures, like the Bhagwadgita, appear to be as relevant today as they were hundreds of years ago. This is because of the fact that these scriptures are built around strands of eternal core knowledge and their main subject is the human being and his problems. Problems need solution, and solution needs true knowledge and its right application. Since the Bhagwadgita shows the faltering humanity the practical insight to its problems and their resolution, it is a hugely popular book even in contemporary times.

Man may vanquish poverty and hunger, but it will take much more for him to vanquish anger, greed, fear and pride. It is exactly here that the divine message of the Bhagwadgita proves useful.

It is hoped that this exposition of the core verses of the Bhagwadgita will put modern humans in the right perspective to deal with the issues confronting them daily—issues which seem to be growing more complex by the day. It is hoped that this will help enhance mental peace and happiness of humans, which are their ultimate objectives.

Acknowledgements

My heartfelt acknowledgements are due to the following persons for their priceless contribution in the accomplishment of this work:

Members of the Arya Samaj, Vasant Kunj community, for their motivation and support.

My wife Bindu for her unstinted encouragement to help me pursue my passions.

Elina Majumdar, Managing Editor at Rupa Publications, for her invaluable guidance in finalizing the manuscript.

Sneha Choudhury, Copy Editor, and other production staff at Rupa Publications.